Strong Words

Strong Words 2019

The best of the Landfall Essay Competition

Selected by Emma Neale

OTAGO UNIVERSITY PRESS
Te Whare Tā o Te Wānanga o Ōtākou

Published by Otago University Press
Te Whare Tā o Te Wānanga o Ōtākou
Level 1, 398 Cumberland Street
Dunedin, New Zealand
university.press@otago.ac.nz
www.otago.ac.nz/press

First published 2019
Copyright © individual authors as listed on page 5

The moral rights of the authors have been asserted.

ISBN 978-1-98-853177-9

Design/layout: Fiona Moffat
Author photograph: Jim Tannock

Cover: *FrenchBayDarkly … #3*, John Reynolds, 2017, oil paint marker on acrylic on canvas, 152cm x 217cm

Printed in China through Asia Pacific Offset

Contents

EMMA NEALE

Introduction

As a first-time judge for the Landfall Essay Competition in 2018, I struggled mightily to deliver a shortlist to the publisher, as so many of the 90 essays entered deserved a wider readership. Initially, I thought this was just being a new-kid-on-the-block, experiencing speed wobbles on my rollerskates as I adapted to the context, and that the standard would inevitably be higher than, say, a fundraising poetry competition. Very few people confuse the formality of an essay with the unstructured outpouring of intense emotion that often appears in community-outreach or charitable-cause writing contests.

I knew the essay competition would chiefly attract driven, passionate and experienced writers; and that winnowing the best from the almost-best was going to tie my dendrites into the kind of contortionist knots we expect of earphone wires. So I was delighted when Rachel Scott, co-publisher at Otago University Press, suggested that there could actually be a book in my struggle. (Not exactly Knausgård, but 'battle' is too military; so let's leave the pun and forge on. All the authors published herein must have high tolerance for this kind of micro-analysis of word choice.) There was hardly a semi-tone off-key in the selected essays.

The range of work entered—and, I gather, in earlier competitions also—suggests that the local literary scene is teeming with perspicacious, perceptive, thoughtful essayists. We'd be delighted if *Strong Words 2019* was the first in a regular series to grow out of the Landfall Essay Competition. But for now—like a host doing party introductions—I need to tell you a bit about the individual minds circulating here, trusting that you'll find some you'll want to forge a long-term connection with, hunting down their past publications, or keeping an eye out for future work.

*

In the *New Yorker* of May 2018, Jia Tolentino argued that political and social pressures meant the online boom in personal essays was over. Yet many New Zealand/Aotearoa writers—on the evidence of the Landfall Essay Competition—beg to differ. They still seem to agree with Virginia Woolf's view in 1905 that an essay, brilliant or profound, dealing with anything 'from the immortality of the soul to the rheumatism in your left shoulder … is primarily an expression of personal opinion'.

Even if we accept that an essay's subject, no matter the costume, is the essayist—the genre is immensely protean. It might explore medical crisis, or expound on the diversity of sex lives in aquatic animals. It can collect factual evidence to support a political argument; it can run so seamlessly in poetry's slipstream that it seems camouflaged as poetry itself.

As Woolf says elsewhere, compared to the poem or the novel, the essay is an almost formless form. In 1905 the novel and the poem might have been easier to define—'A novel has a story, a poem rhyme'—but even if we expand our definitions of these, Woolf's question about the essay still holds: '… but what art can the essayist use in these short lengths of prose to sting us wide awake and fix us in a trance which is not sleep but rather an intensification of life?'

In other words, there is not much an essay *must* have. It doesn't need a narrative; it doesn't need prosody or line breaks; it doesn't even need an argument. It can be, in the words of one of our most prominent new essayists, Ashleigh Young, an existential meditation, an exploration of shifting angles, something that can enact the way a mind shapes thought.

That last quality is something poetry excels at, too. When it comes to spotting genres from the post-postmodern cycle lane, it can feel as if we're trapped on a roundabout, never able to make a smooth, non-perilous exit out of a circular argument.

So what exactly was I looking for?

By the time I had read about 60 essays that adhered to the idea that the self was the true subject, I began to want work that could also use the experience as a gateway to travel elsewhere; as a way into understanding a culture, a social climate, a time, a common experience. The catch even then, of course, is that style and craft had to be smooth, the 'argument' or opinion backed up with crisp and credible evidence; the link between, say, historical incident and current social phenomena a comparison that sings in the same register—comparing apples to apple pies, not oranges to swivel chairs.

Entries in the 2018 Landfall Essay Competition featured a radiant spectrum of often deeply affecting topics.

Alice Miller's winning essay, 'The Great Ending', on World War One and the armistice, manages to pick out both telling and comic detail that illuminates the past, and also to summarise a mood and an era. The balance she achieves, and the poetic tone she attains, make reading her essay feel so different to the memories I have of trudging through the textbooks I tried to read as a teenager, as a result of which I made the deeply regrettable decision not to study history formally. Alice Miller's deceptively light and agile style manages to be both informative and sharply moving, as does the way she lets the idiosyncratic, the apparently frivolous, the unfamiliar, sit down quietly beside the tragically altered and the massive, terrifying cogs of war and political conflict. The way the essay deftly flick flacks between things as disparate as 'ladies' hosiery', children's games, burning effigies of the Kaiser, declarations of the end of civilisation and spiritual revelations, shows us the immense range and variety of human feeling. Alice Miller's work impressed with its teeming yet elegantly controlled catalogue of international and national, Pākehā and Māori historical events; for the lyricism of the prose which glides from moments of understated comedy to those of stark horror. All the contraries are held in a delicate web that says we humans contain and withstand multitudes; that out of our shared and personal history we struggle and try to rise; that we are composed of innocence and futility, vision and foolishness, tragedy and desire.

In second place was Susan Wardell's breath-stopping work, 'Shining Through the Skull'. I admired its ability to confront personal qualities and choices with such an unforgiving eye; to be confessional—to seriously study identity—without veering into the prurience and narcissism of TMI social media posts and feeds that can leave the reader feeling used and ground down. The essay glints with poetry as it also touches on a number of potent themes, darting away again in a manner that emphasises the burning coals beneath: ambition, religion, vanity, charity, privacy, exploitation, the pitfalls in the anonymity of the internet, consent, shame, sexual fetishes.

Sam Keenan's essay 'Bad Girls', on teenage sexuality, transgression, the expectations of and dictates to female children in the 1980s, when second-wave feminism tried to empower young women at the same time that society still often blamed them for encouraging or inviting male abuse and violence—has a poignant sense of retrospective understanding, of only fully seeing some constrictions with the wisdom and long view that time lends. It gives a sense of how some fears and habits can be not only a natural aspect of differing personalities, but also so deeply imprinted by the social climate of our youth that they are never fully shaken off. Keenan's essay is understated yet powerfully affecting, perhaps particularly to another reader shaped by the 80s, when we asserted equality at the same time as fighting off lecherous bosses, strangers, relatives, friends-of-the-family, colleagues; rapists, abusers. The #metoo movement has made many women reflect hard on their own experiences, and decide whether or not to confront the abusers of their past—if those perpetrators are still alive. The essay made me wonder whether young women will always have to temper their urge for freedom with a precautionary approach, or whether the issues raised in this essay will one day become alien and purely historical in a highly welcome sense.

Comedy seemed rare in the submissions. Perhaps the word 'essay' makes writers want to put on their formal wear, like old Oxbridge dons in their teaching gowns—and for that reason Tobias Buck's lovely study of a small-town sauna and its role as 'psychological pressure valve' and site of 'temporary casual integration' as an antidote to disconnection and winter blues was a welcome respite. There are some affectionate and wry character portraits—'Conversation with Tony is serious and endlessly varied as long as you enjoy talking about whitebait'—and a gathering sense that the vulnerability of disrobing for a steam can produce both an urge to confess and also, perhaps, greater tolerance for others. 'Though dissenting in close quarters might cross your mind, this is usually outweighed by a more egalitarian need to simply interact and allow someone to be, even momentarily, heard.'

Two vivid essays on pain made me experience a weird sub-species of *Schadenfreude*—shakily almost appreciative that Bryan Walpert and Tracey Slaughter have both experienced their different afflictions—because the experiences have had such electric expression. In Walpert's case it is accompanied by a sardonic sense of humour and an implicit criticism of 'appearance fascism'; in Slaughter's by a searing lyricism. Tracey Slaughter discusses how language fails in the face of physical pain, particularly in reaching certain doctors she encountered; yet it reaches the reader so acutely that I found I could only read this essay in small bursts; as if I had to rebuild the ability to bear the agony and isolation it describes. At the end, the cry from the valley of pain becomes paradoxically almost as joyous as a child's kite flown on a cold, windy day. It reminds me of Katherine Mansfield's line (which I've had pinned to my study wall since my father died)—'Hanging in our little cages over the gulf of eternity, we must sing—sing.'

Tim Upperton's elegant and easy glide from stepping stone to stepping stone of the concealed and the revealed—ranging from insect life to the secrets of another person's thoughts, and the layers of mystery in certain poems—is a meander where every apparent digression actually gets us closer to a source of light. His essay seems as if it should enjoy rubbing shoulders here with equally moving pieces by John Allison and Fiona Clark, which—among other topics—also bear witness to the healing strangeness of poetry, its ministering use of both music and silence.

While it might seem obvious that a judge and editor who writes poetry would be drawn to excellent essays on literary subjects (such as those by both Derek Schulz and Louise Slocombe), I was also hungry for work that could shred the veil of my own reading habits and preconceptions; essays that could expose the world in a new skin. Work by several other authors did exactly that: Justine Whitfield, Madeleine Child, P.J. Stanley, Jocelyn Prasad, Kirsteen Ure, Mikaela Nyman, Jane Blaikie, Cait Kneller. Every one of these writers has filtered into my thoughts as I've moved from desk to errand to chores over the months since first reading these authors. I've found myself revisiting everything, from the subtle, compressed expression of loss, the stunning, clear-eyed lyricism of 'Pūriri Moth', to the more thunderous and sometimes satirical rhetoric of Jessica Maclean as she explores the nature of time and identity from a bicultural perspective; to the links between mother, culture, craft and clothing in Jocelyn Prasad's 'Uncut Cloth', to the tension between ecological guilt and economic exigency, personal boundaries and the human need for touch in Justine Whitfield's 'The Klimt Bubbles: Contemplating concealment and connection'.

The other authors here have made me puzzle over the nature of bilingualism and the role of song; the scrim (and crims) behind the walls of national myths; the ongoing effort to fit in socially; the painful and persistent psychological contrail of addiction; the quirks and fascinations of scientific obsession; or the bewilderment and dislocation of being cast out by a parent because of religion, and over where religions shade into cults—and about how even in apparently diffident Aotearoa New Zealand, religion often both still shapes many lives, and splinters families.

There's a vivid, varied and sometimes confronting gallery of ideas here. There were more essays that I wanted to include but whose authors were unable to grant us publication rights for various reasons. If your appetites for fine and moving essay writing are sharpened by reading this collection, scout around bookshelves and the internet for Nadine Anne Hura's essay on learning te reo as an adult student; Lynley Edmeades' work on grammar and identity; and Steve Braunias on mangrove swamps and preparing for the apocalypse. Or hold on tight for results from the next Landfall Essay Competition. I'm hopeful that Otago University Press will need to have some more strong words with you.

Emma Neale
July 2019

REFERENCES
from the immortality of the soul … Virginia Woolf, 'The Decay of the Essay'.
but what art can the essayist use … Virgina Woolf, 'The Modern Essay'.
an existential meditation … See Ashleigh Young—5 Questions, 'These Rough Notes – VUP News', 2 August 2016: http://victoriauniversitypress.blogspot.com/2016/08/ashleigh-young-5-questions.html

ALICE MILLER

The Great Ending 1918

1.

The story of the great ending begins with a mistake and ends with a miracle.

On 8 November a century ago, when the announcement came that the Great War was over, it was dusty in Balclutha. Dust from running children, dust from motor cars, dust from men's shoes as their owners ran down the main street, blowing tin whistles. All the townspeople were out of doors. 'It was as if,' a journalist wrote, 'a highly strung violin string had snapped':

> *every bell clanged its utmost, whistles blew incessantly, and every empty petrol tin in the precincts of the town seemed to be called into service. A favourite practice was to tie a string of tins to a motor car or cycle and set off at a good bat up the street. A scratch band was raised, and, with tin whistles, trumpets and sirens, this was an effective, though unmusical, addition to the outburst of sound.*

When the crowd were told that the report was premature—that in fact the Great War had not yet ended, the armistice was still not signed—the mood didn't change. 'The general feeling was that if the armistice was not signed, it jolly well ought to be, seeing that we had gone so far.'

Four days later there was still some uncertainty:

NO NEWS YET
GERMAN SURRENDER CONFIDENTLY PREDICTED
SHOULD GERMANS REFUSE TERMS
WILL BATTER THEM INTO SUBMISSION

—*Otago Daily Times*, 12 November 1918

Thursday's error had made everyone nervous. But by 9am the government confirmed that the armistice was signed at last. The national headlines became bolder: GERMANY OUT OF THE WAR; GREAT WAR ENDED; JOY ALL OVER THE WORLD.

Finally, the real celebrations could commence. In the small, landlocked town of Levin an ambitious two-day programme was planned. The signal would be given by the ringing of all bells, including the firebell and buglers in motor cars. All flags were to be hoisted, and all cars, bicycles and other vehicles to be carefully decollated for the parade. At 3pm the grand procession would assemble in Post Office Square.

The procession was ordered into fourteen groups, beginning with RETURNED SOLDIERS in uniform, followed shortly after by TRAINING FARM BOYS and PATRIOTIC AND RED CROSS WOMEN. The last two groups in the procession were NATIVES IN NATIVE COSTUME and CITIZENS IN DECORATED CARS.

But that Monday, the end of the war was not the only news. From London came the report that a game of soldiers' rugby football between Australia Headquarters and New Zealand Headquarters had been won by New Zealand.

A steamer travelling from San Francisco to Manila had been struck by lightning. Forty out of forty-six of the crew were missing.

Closer to home, Mrs M. Moody of 69 Roxburgh Street 'was walking along Lambton-quay, just outside the Gear Company's shop, when she slipped and fell, fracturing her left leg. John Condon, a fireman on the ferry steamer, fell in Abel Smith-street and suffered severe concussion by striking his head on the pavement.'

And in Vulcan Lane in Auckland, the well-known secretary of the Takapuna Jockey Club was knocked down by a four-seater motor car. The car stopped with one of its front wheels resting on the man's abdomen. A number of bystanders helped to lift the car, and the secretary was rapidly extricated from underneath. His clothing was severely torn and he was dazed; however, his cigar remained lit and he continued to smoke.

There was another problem, that Monday, that overshadowed all others.

At one of Auckland's largest private hotels most of the staff were struck down by influenza, to the extent that several very distinguished guests took over the duties of the domestic servants. Some guests had to make their own beds.

There was even the very odd spectacle of a titled gentleman working the lift.

Māori settlements in the north were badly hit by the epidemic. In many regions, hospitals were overflowing and schools were rapidly converted into hospitals. Many appointments were postponed, including the Church of England annual sale, a card evening at the Bell Tea rooms, and the fancy-dress ball of the Arowhenua Maori Soldier Day Committee.

Lemons became wildly expensive. People of means were requested to donate citrus fruit. Those with motor cars were asked to lend them to the effort.

Schools were closed, as were moving picture theatres and ordinary theatres, dancing halls, billiard saloons, concert rooms and shooting galleries.

Children's demonstrations on Armistice Day were also postponed.

What stayed open late were chemists' shops. The shops quickly ran out of bottles, and urged the public to bring their own. They also requested that nobody follow the example of one particular (unnamed) lady, who ran into the chemist at the height of the epidemic, demanding cosmetic face powder.

Strangely, it was people in their twenties and thirties who were most susceptible to the influenza virus. Soldiers returned from months of foreign battle only to die from the flu. After death, bodies often turned dark purple or black.

Levin's Peace Programme, however, remained unaffected; influenza or not, the show would go on. Day Two of the Peace Programme consisted of a sports gathering and district picnic, all held at the Levin Park Domain, with numerous attractions including a Punch and Judy Show. Hot water, tea, milk and sugar were provided free of charge on the grounds. Guests brought their lunch, along with the family teapot.

The Fisk Jubilee Singers were still scheduled to sing at the Oddfellows' Hall on 13 November, with a programme featuring 'popular airs' and 'coon songs'.

The *Otago Daily Times* offered a useful suggestion for 'when you get into a frame of mind that makes life seem one tiresome duty after another'. The suggested product promised to 'tone up the entire system, help make the blood rich and red, strengthen the nerves, increase the appetite, put colour in the cheeks and lips, and drive away that unnatural feeling'. Just ask for Dr Williams' Pink Pills for Pale People.

A writer to the *Auckland Star* suggested that when a son reaches a 'critical age', a father should 'place in his hands a standard book of advice to young men, and let the mother act likewise for the daughter'. This being done, children will receive 'necessary knowledge re. their sexual nature … in a safe and thorough manner'.

On the evening of Day Two of Levin's Peace Programme all shops were lit up. There was a monster torchlight procession from the post office at 7pm, a free impromptu concert, and the burning of an effigy of the Kaiser.

Towns everywhere had rigged up their own effigies, some adorned with an iron cross and 'ignominiously dangled'. The Kaiser was doused in petrol and set alight, and the townspeople cheered as he burned.

Lloyd George was quoted in the newspapers:

> In the spring we were being sorely pressed. The Channel ports were being threatened. The enemy steel was pointed at our hearts. It is now autumn. Constantinople is almost within gunfire. Austria is shattered and broken. The Kaiser and Crown Prince have abdicated, and a successor has not been found, but a regency proclaimed. This is the greatest judgment in history. Germany has a choice to-day, but she will have none to-morrow. She is ruined inside and outside …

> Our terms must prevent a recurrence … Let us banish faction. It would be unwise to forget. We must impose justice, Divine justice, which is the foundation of civilisation … We are not going to repeat the folly of 1870.

In a letter to the editor, H.S. protested that while it was a fineable offence to discharge firearms, it would be found in the suburbs that there were more and more small boys with pea-rifles. The boys and their rifles were a regular commotion. It was well time these children's irresponsible parents were fined. The government must put a true end to the 'pea-rifle nuisance'.

Ladies' high-grade soft white hose were for sale: seamless; the best; all sizes; at the sale price of three shillings and one penny (postage two shillings extra).

The *Taranaki Daily News* announced that flouncings were in style once again. Morey's had a fine range of flouncing embroideries for ladies.

2.

Meanwhile, in Europe, *The Decline of the West* (*Der Untergang des Abendlandes*) was published. In it, Oswald Spengler argued that the Western world was at its end and we were witnessing its final season—winter—before a new historical cycle. According to Herr Spengler:

> The era of individualism, liberalism and democracy, of humanitarianism and freedom, is nearing its end. The masses will accept with resignation the victory of the Caesars, the strong men, and will obey them.

Irish poet W.B. Yeats also believed that the world was operating on a cycle. In 1918 he and his wife were channelling spirits. Their proposed cycle was just over a thousand years long and divided into twelve sections. According to the Yeats' notes, in 1875 a period of 'war and abstractions' began. This lasted until 1927, with the 'elimination of intellect, Europe in artificial unity' (although this phrase ended with a question mark). Around 2050 there would be 'adoration of force, decadence'.

The Yeats' research on these cycles would appear in one of his poems the following year. In early drafts of the poem, Yeats addressed the war directly— 'the Germans are … now to Russia come'. He cut this line in his revision. The final version ended: 'And what rough beast, its hour come round at last,/ Slouches towards Bethlehem to be born?'

In Shrewsbury, England, on Armistice Day, the mother of Wilfred Edward Salter Owen—the young man who wrote 'In all my dreams, before my helpless sight,/ He plunges at me, guttering, choking, drowning'—received a telegram. The telegram said that regrettably, Wilfred had been killed fighting in France. He was twenty-five years old. When his mother received the telegram he had already been dead a week.

In neutral Switzerland the young Jorges Luis Borges had graduated from the Collège de Genève. 'You have wakened,' he would write, 'not out of sleep, but into a prior dream.'

3.

How would New Zealanders remember the war? The *Evening Post* suggested it would be recalled as the point when all women started smoking. Smokers included women frequenting great hotels and restaurants, but also those doing 'men's work'. 'Observe,' the journalist wrote, 'the habitual readiness and insouciance with which they whisk the case from pocket, close it with a snap, and lightly tap the cigarette on the back of the left hand before lighting up.'

Should we mention that when the armistice was announced in Albany, it was the thirty-first week of the second egg-laying competition? Or that the Williamstown Cup was won by *Seabound*, beating *Red Signal* by a neck?

There is one last story to remember, which was not reported in the papers. It happened on the day of the first, false armistice, 8 November.

On that afternoon a man witnessed a strange cloud, like a whirlwind, come towards him. He ran back towards his farmhouse and felt something press heavily on his shoulders. He claimed he could see, stretching towards him, every one of the world's roads.

When he entered his family's house he couldn't speak. But something spoke through him: 'May peace be upon you,' the voice said. 'I am the Holy Spirit who is speaking to you; wash yourselves clean, make yourselves ready.'

The man cleared out his house and instructed others to do the same. He claimed to speak through the Holy Spirit or the archangel Gabriel or Michael. His family were not the only ones to believe he had gone mad. He took them walking over rough farmland at night, stumbling over piles of dirt. He separated out selected family members' belongings, and said they belonged to the dead.

Those whose belongings he separated out caught influenza and died. The ones he urged to leave their houses stayed alive. People began to listen.

While across the country a false armistice was celebrated, on the man's farm the healing began. First a dying man, after prayer, saw a needle emerge from his thigh and was cured. A girl who was bedridden walked again. By the end of 1918 Ratana's farm would have had many, many visitors—and 8 November was remembered as a day of revelation.

Shortly before his death, Jorges Luis Borges said to a hall of people: 'We do not read to discover the end. After all, people reread stories, so it is impossible to believe they read to discover how they will end.'

And in this great ending we have our interruptions, starts; a mistake and a miracle. Premature announcements and divine revelations, a terrible illness and the promise of healing, straw men we string up and burn. Days of unfortunate falls, of women pressing cigarettes to insouciant lips, of flouncing and miracle pills and the stacking of blue bodies. Days when we shoot our pea-rifles into our neighbour's garden, and with strange clouds ahead, sing as loudly as we can, of dust that builds on dust.

REFERENCES
1.
All the townspeople …; The general feeling was … 'Triumph's Tocsin', *Clutha Leader*, 12 November 1918.

Four days later … 'No news yet', *Otago Daily Times*, 12 November 1918.

The national headlines … 'Germany out of the war', *Evening Post*, 12 November 1918; 'The Great War ended', *Horowhenua Chronicle*, 12 November 1918.

Finally, the real celebrations … 'Levin's peace programme', *Horowhenua Chronicle*, 12 November 1918.

From London came the report … 'Football', *Wanganui Chronicle*, 12 November 1918.

A steamer travelling … 'Struck by lightning', *Marlborough Express*, 12 November 1918.

Closer to home … 'Two accidents', *Evening Post*, 12 November 1918.

And in Vulcan Lane …; At one of Auckland's … 'Local and general', *Evening Post*, 12 November 1918.

Māori settlements … 'Many residents attacked', *New Zealand Herald*, 12 November 1918.

Many appointments were postponed … 'Town & country', *Timaru Herald*, 12 November 1918.

Lemons became wildly … 'Clothing, fruit, cars', *Auckland Star*, 12 November 1918; 'The influenza epidemic', *Auckland Star*, 12 November 1918.

Schools were closed … 'Places of amusement closed', *Evening Post*, 12 November 1918.

Children's demonstrations … 'No children's gatherings', *Evening Post*, 12 November 1918.

What stayed open late … 'Bring your own bottle', *Evening Post*, 12 November 1918.

Strangely, it was people … James Belich, *Paradise Reforged* (London: Penguin, 2002); Molly Billings, 'The Influenza Epidemic': http://virus.stanford.edu/uda/

Levin's peace programme … 'Levin's peace programme', *Horowhenua Chronicle*, 12 November 1918.

The Fisk Jubilee Singers … 'Local and general', *Akaroa Mail and Banks Peninsula Advertiser*, 12 November 1918.

The *Otago Daily Times* offered … 'Pale Pills', *Otago Daily Times*, 12 November 1918.

A writer to the *Auckland Star* … 'Children's morals', *Auckland Star*, 12 November 1918.

On the evening of Day Two … 'Levin's peace programme', *Horowhenua Chronicle*, 12 November 1918.

Towns everywhere had rigged up … 'Prohibition in practice', *Taranaki Daily News*, 12 November 1918; 'Triumph's Tocsin', *Clutha Leader*, 12 November 1918.

Lloyd George was quoted … 'Germany ruined', *Auckland Star*, 12 November 1918.

In a letter to the editor … 'The pea-rifle nuisance', *Auckland Star*, 12 November 1918.

Ladies' high-grade soft white hose … 'Untitled', *Otago Daily Times*, 12 November 1918.

The *Taranaki Daily News* announced … 'Local and general', *Taranaki Daily News*, 12 November 1918.

2.

Meanwhile in Europe … Oswald Spengler, *The Decline of the West*, 2 vols, trans. Charles Francis Atkinson (New York: Alfred A. Knopf, 1922).

The Irish poet … William Butler Yeats, *The Collected Works of W.B. Yeats Volume XIII: A vision* (New York: Simon & Schuster, 2013).

The Yeats' research … Terence Brown, *The Literature of Ireland: Culture and criticism* (Cambridge: Cambridge University Press, 2010), p. 85.

In Shrewsbury, England … 'Wilfred Owen's Shrewsbury home granted Grade II listing', *Guardian*, 29 December 2014.

In neutral Switzerland … Jorges Luis Borges, *The Aleph*, trans. Andrew Hurley (New York: Penguin, 2004).

3.

The *Evening Post* suggested … 'Women smokers', *Evening Post*, 12 November 1918.

Should we mention that … 'Egg-laying competition', *New Zealand Herald*, 12 November 1918.

Or that the Williamstown Cup … 'Williamstown Cup', *Evening Post*, 12 November 1918.

On that afternoon … Angela Ballara, 'Ratana, Tahupotiki Wiremu', from the Dictionary of New Zealand Biography: www.TeAra.govt.nz/en/biographies/3r4/ratana-tahupotiki-wiremu

First a dying man … Morrison, Paterson and Rae Knowles, *Mana Māori and Christianity* (Wellington: Huia, 2012).

Shortly before his death … George Watson, 'An Unquenchable Gaiety of Mind', *American Scholar*, 31 May 2012.

SUSAN WARDELL

Shining Through the Skull

The fontanelle is the most terrifying part of a newborn baby. My daughter was born with no hair—the merest hint of red-gold fuzz. I ran my fingers over her head, over the basin in the middle of her skull where bones did not yet meet. The site of her sentience. The skin there was hot with its own central pulse. A person I did not know yet, thrumming under my fingers. I could not breathe.

I was also born bald, and I have chosen to be made bald twice more: once for a cheering and charitable crowd, and once for an invisible audience I was too naïve to see.

I'll tell you about the first time I shaved my head. I was sixteen and the leader of my school's Christian group—an introverted, bass-playing overachiever with plans to save the world. The long, dark hair flowed all the way down my back. I'd been growing it since kindergarten. I arranged the fundraiser with the local branch of CanTeen; made up some flimsy collection boxes by cutting slots into butter containers. A few shops around town agreed to put them on the counter. I took one to my school's office, my picture, loose-haired and half-smiling, taped to it. The principal's eyebrows hit the ceiling. 'Oh no, Susan, you shouldn't mutilate yourself like that!' I still remember the flush of shame, pulling my sleeves down over the year-old scars on my arms. 'There are other ways to fundraise, surely?'

'It's a slap in the face to people who really have cancer,' a favourite teacher cornered me in the hallway to say. I cried in the bathroom where I used to go with the yellow craft knife I had stolen from a friend. A third teacher had to allay my obvious distress by checking with a student a year below me who did have cancer. I received a blessing by proxy. But by then I knew the school didn't want a head girl with a 'mutilated' head, and that was a mantle I had hoped for.

I've always been an all-or-nothing kind of person. But extremes are not just about the more, they're also about the less. How low can I go? How much can

I lose? When I was fourteen I wanted to be a martyr. I cherished a little book about the young people who had died at Columbine, Christ's name on their lips. I used to have dreams about being stood on a brick wall with a gun to my head. So in my dramatic teen mind, the time had come. I took a deep breath and followed through. Besides, the cool girls had started talking to me, whispering disbelief and solidarity in the hallways. I collected a paltry hundred dollars in gold coins. But if I am honest, the money had never been the point.

On the big day I wore my favourite pink top and a string of cheap pearls. I sat between two strangers on a temporary stage in front of the railway station. There was a small crowd. My hair did not fall on the makeshift flooring that morning—it was divided and carefully tied, sliced off one little pigtail at a time. The neat locks were bagged up for a wig-maker. The final buzz was exhilarating. I felt reborn. I walked away grinning. Did you know that air has a texture? As I moved through the mild morning, I felt as if I were swimming through it. Like it had ripples, a grain. The next morning I stood up the front of my small church hall to lead the music, and I did not bow my head in prayer. Instead I tilted my face to the sky and felt God pour light down into my naked skull. Later my pastor told me it had been moving to see me up there like that. And so I moved out of my own body and into his eyes, and liked the view.

On the street it was different. I felt guilty walking around town. What if strangers thought I had cancer? What right did I have to withdraw from that bank of public sympathies? I flew to a family wedding in Auckland with my dad. He phoned ahead to make sure no one thought I was dying, and I figured that at least then they wouldn't be talking about my parents' separation. But at the last moment I lost my nerve, searching my drawers for the thick dark wig my mum had once used to dress as Cleopatra. I itched and sweated all day. At the end of the night I took it off and felt amazing, sitting in the sparkling candlelight, free and bare. I danced with my father. I learned that being hairless could make me feel fearless.

My hair grew back. Hair does that. But that was only the first shave.

It was six years later, and I had wasted no time. I had studied and graduated with first-class honours. I had travelled with my best friend to volunteer at the edge of a war zone—seeking better stories, and very nearly getting them. We missed out on a massacre in South Sudan by a mere 40km. I've milked that story a lot over the years. I don't tend to mention that we spent a good portion of the trip reading Christian romance novels and arguing over our one jar of peanut butter.

Back home I slipped compunctiously back into a middle-class student life. Then one day I got an email from my friend Regina. Regina who had real stories, who had fled Sudan as a child and grown up in a refugee camp. One of the sweetest, most self-effacing, hard-working people I've ever met, who now wanted to pursue development studies so she could go back home and help people. I had no money to respond. But I didn't fret long before I had the brilliant thought. My flatmate had recently made a big pile of cash shaving her head. There had been an advertisement on Student Job Search. I emailed someone called Justin who was 'overseas at present' but was willing to arrange it through his local contacts. They would pay me $800 to first film an 'unconventional' cut and then to do a full buzz. They would also have a photographer take pictures of the results for a 'beauty positive' alopecia awareness campaign. $800 goes a long way in South Sudan. I quickly set a date.

On the day I climbed an old staircase squeezed in between two storefronts. The photography studio above had a four-poster bed in one corner for boudoir shoots. The hairdresser was chatty and professional. I was wearing a black cocktail dress and heels, as instructed, and reminding myself that I'd done this before. Well, not exactly this. The hair fell to polished wood, and there was no applause.

I am not a hero, but I like to feel like a martyr. As my hair fell there, I imagined it falling at the feet of the worthiest woman in Africa. I suppose I hoped it would fit me for battle, bear me back into the 'good fight' alongside her. I have had a tendency to borrow the afflictions of others. I have a tendency to wear them as my own.

After the clippers came a new offer—an extra $100 if I got my head shaved back to smooth with cream and a razor. The procedure was specific: I had to request it on camera. I left with my skull cold and 'smoother than a newborn rat'.

I proudly sent the money, with no specifics on its origin.

Regina was the one who taught me to cook beans. We had just two large pots, tended carefully over a tiny open fire, in an IDP camp in the middle of the

23

savannah land. She didn't laugh or *tsk* when I burned the *mondazzi*. She called me 'sister' and patiently braided my wayward *mundu* hair. My head burned for two days with the tight twists she made so close to my scalp, and at night I lay awake beside her, determined not to say anything. I wanted so much to be her sister. It was only a couple of months after the second shave that I went back to East Africa, this time to do research for my doctorate. Great timing, I thought. Extremely practical for the heat. But I was working in the city this time, where I was dismayed to find the educated young Pentecostals I hoped to make friends with all had glossy, salon-treated hair. I stood up the front with an inch of un-styled fuzz and looked positively, paradoxically, poor. 'God will lead you to your place of prosperity,' the pastors preached while giving a side-eye to my obvious lack of … faith? Femininity? Virtue?

> *… but that if a woman has long hair, it is her glory? For long hair is given to her as a covering.* —1 Corinthians 11:15 (NLT)

Back home in the Anthropology Department, one of the other postgrads was also writing about Pentecostal women and what she called 'biblical feminism'.[2] She herself had left a fundamentalist background in the USA, started wearing trousers, cut her hair short, and then gone back to study them.

> *For if a woman does not cover her head, she might as well have her hair cut off; but if it is a disgrace for a woman to have her hair cut off or her head shaved, then she should cover her head.* —1 Corinthians 11:6 (NIV)

She told me about the women from United Pentecostal Church International who grow their hair sometimes to ankle length, even suffering back problems from its weight. Their uncut hair not only represents their faith but gives them authority to 'charge angels'—to make requests at the throne of God, to drape it over the sick and claim healing. As I listened I imagined those women, honey-lit in mid-western churches, praying (silently) as glory streams down their dark blonde mantles. Like fire, like melted amber. In my mind they became stained glass windows: *in memoriam*.

My husband tells a story about falling in love with the back of my head. I sat in front of him in a church pew at a youth group study night. We were fifteen and my hair was long and dark. When I planned to shave my head for a second time I was twenty-two and we were married. I asked him what he thought. He shrugged: 'It's your body.' In bed, after the deed was done, he gently ran his hand over the militant black fuzz that remained. We were both testing this out: the change, the thing gone, the thing revealed. 'That feels strange,' I told him. The tiny barbs velcroed to the pillow when I slept, sexless. It was a while before we learned the truth.

It happened on a car trip. I was chatting with a friend who had shaved her head not long after me. With the same people, in fact, and at my referral. It came up in conversation … or came out, I should say. The ongoing emails. The online chats at odd hours. The uncomfortable questions. I'd been trying to politely ignore them for a couple of years by then. Starting with the email from 'Nicole', who was a stylist in town, wanting to ask if I would shave again. Offering me $1000. I declined. Then the magazine editors who wanted to shoot me for a cutting-edge cover: $1500 was mentioned. Then came salon owners planning a big live opening: $10,000. I exchanged a few emails. 'Just in case it's real,' I told my husband. No charitable impulse this time, when we had just $14 across all our accounts. The money had been real last time. But time wore on and nothing came of it until one day Justin offered to pay me again, for another head shave, another photo shoot. By then I'd had enough and politely (always politely) refused. He asked why I chose to get the first shave done. Whether I'd opted for the razor shave. When I said I couldn't remember, he sent me a screenshot from the video, where the hairdresser is poised above my bowed and newly bald head with a razor. My stomach felt strange.

'Is this you?' he asked.

'I have to go. I have an early start tomorrow.'

'Did you like the feeling of the blade on your head?'

You know those hairless cats that people enter into shows? Sphynx, the breed is called, with sloped eyes and folds upon folds of flesh in a pale, foetal pink. Axolotl pink. The pink of something dragged out of the dark, in the maw of something worse still.

It's not that there were *no* warning bells, you see, it's just that it's easy to get used to small fires. My friend's exchanges with these people were even more obviously 'off', I comforted myself by thinking. 'Do you usually shave your armpits?' they asked her. 'What do you use to shave your body hair?' She shut down the conversations much more quickly than I did.

Is this what happens when women talk to each other? When we pause our incessant, brave, blind 'just getting on with it'? 'What, you too?' we ask in surprise.

'Yes. Me too.'

Of course we began to wonder how many more women were out there. Where the images were really being sent. I considered making a file of all the messages and all the details we knew. Taking it to the police. But was there a crime? We had consented. (How much does one have to know to consent?) We had been paid. (Where is the line between exploitation and commerce?) Our hair was by then in cute shoulder-length bobs.

Besides, I was preoccupied with watching myself expand, encompass. Hearing my daughter's heartbeat, like the rush of little waves, inside the ocean of me. I left it at an uncomfortable curiosity. I got on with my life.

In the end the story found me before I found it. I opened my laptop one day and read the headlines: 'Dunedin student feels violated after finding picture on fetish website' and 'Bald backpacker funder plays down fetish connection'. I couldn't believe it. And yet, I completely could. The full scope of the operation never emerged; nor did the person behind an email chain from 'Gemma' to 'Muhammed' to 'Justin'. The story was much the same as mine among the few women the reporters talked to.

I broke the rule and read the comments. One anonymous pundit confirmed that it was 'pretty obvious' and 'the way the ad reads is definitely sketchy'. You'd have to be 'dumb as a stump' not to tweak to it being for a fetish website, someone else says. My chest tightens, reading this. Writing it now. I remind myself that I finished my PhD at age twenty-five. That I've won awards. Been published. I remind myself of this and yet my chest stays tight. 'It's not like they even had to get their tits out, so I can't see why there would be any shame really,' another random commentator confirms. Yes. Yes. My mind swims around and around that pool of revelation, looking for the tap left on. The source of the shame. I can't seem to find it. I just know I'm swimming in it.

Did I mention that I liked the photos they took of me? I put them on Facebook. I thought I looked fierce and beautiful—lips pinked, lashes long, head unapologetically bare and tilted curiously at the camera. They had posed me well. I have always enjoyed posing. They were classy photos. But dark roots soon reclaimed the bare skin.

Am I wounded? I don't think so. Embarrassed? Yes, that. The line between innocence and naivety is purple and taut. It is vanity that shames me. That I'd thought I was the cover-girl and ended up the pin-up girl, or something less than that. That people I don't know are panting as they watch my head being slowly bared. They are probably paying for it. I wonder how much.

'What do you notice first about a person when you meet them?' I remember a friend asking a group of us, perched around a bench outside our imposing brick high school. We were thirteen, priming ourselves for this new kind of noticing and being noticed. 'Eyes,' someone says. Others agree. 'Confidence,' someone else adds. 'Hair' is the honest, simple answer I would not speak. The first thing I would notice. Blonde, brunette, redhead. (Did my inner monologue read like a bad joke?) Short, long. Curly, straight. Bald.

What is it about baldness that is so titillating? I wonder now. Can the fetishists even explain it themselves? As if desire comes with a roadmap through the synapses. Over the skin. In primary school I resolved that I wanted to be beautiful, not hot. I had a feel of 'beautiful' that I couldn't yet communicate. It was something to do with swans and flowers. Gowns and long hair. It was clean and pale as the moon.

Now the pale moon of my head brought a rise to a stranger through the screen. What's that to me? What does it matter? Would I still have considered it if I knew the purpose of those photos? If I was paid more? Do I regret it? I don't know. Or perhaps I just can't answer, even to myself. In her poem 'Hairless', Jo Shapcott questions whether the bald can lie. 'The nature of the skin says not,' she answers:

> it's newborn-pale, erection-tender stuff,
> every thought visible—pure knowledge,
> mind in action—shining through the skull.

I imagine myself seated at a large dinner table with a group of bald women. Joan of Arc sits to my left, a wine glass cocked in her long hands. Jo March is on my right, sampling cheese. Fantine sits across from us, applying black lipstick, as Furiosa makes everyone laugh with biting comments about politicians.

27

Grace Jones beside her, already quite drunk, is snorting as she makes a small monument with the salt shakers. Evey smiles, her mouth wide. We drink and laugh. We plan a revolution of proud, shaved women walking tall through bloody streets. The wine spills.

What is it about bare skin that always recalls violence? Is it the implication of a blade? Or simply the paring down of the ornamental, like the ritualised removal of garments, of jewellery, before a fight: 'Jesus, hold my earrings!'[3] The shedding of personal identifiers that make it easier to harm, easier to be harmed.

On my first visit to the Human Anatomy museum it is the eyelashes that get me. The eyelashes and other places where the skin is left on. The knuckles where thick gold hair loops in tiny tensile arches against cavernous pores. A face, in citrine sections, where one corner slice bears a five o'clock shadow. Frozen at 5pm now for five years. Fifteen years. More. I wonder whose job it is to shave the dead.

The job of poetry is to make beautiful what we cannot bear to know. To tell the truth, shorn and holy. But as the poet said, humankind cannot bear very much reality. The job of a woman's hair is to style and fuss over the top of what we cannot bear to see: her raw, corporeal self, so often stripped against her will. At the end of the Second World War, French women accused of collaborating with or sleeping with German soldiers were stripped and beaten and their heads shaved. No trial, just mob justice. They were called les femmes tondues—the shorn women.

I do not know what it is liked to be stripped against my will. By illness. By enemies. By friends. Yet for a time, I too was a shorn woman: defined by what I lacked.

There is a horrible vulnerability in a bare head, with its so-thin dermis and the dark pound of blood so near the surface. Head wounds always bleed a lot. They won't keep quiet.

So, what of the choice to bare oneself on purpose? To fiercely pre-empt the violence of the world? I think of the protests where women walk naked down the street. Each bare step claims 'I am safe here.' I see their photos in my stream and still some part of me just wants to wrap them in blankets. They look cold and soft, even with brave chins tilted, hands busy with signs that say (without words): 'You can't touch me.' But I'm afraid, so afraid, that that's not true.

She is clothed with strength and dignity, and she laughs without fear of the future —Proverbs 21:35

Britney Spears' shave is said to be a marker of her sad decline into mental disarray. Grace Jones' bald head is heralded as a radical rejection of mainstream femininity. It's only when we shave our own heads that we are dangerous— pitiable or powerful. Shaved against our will, we are easier to make into saints or whores. Or both. Indeed, Fantine's final 'choice' to take to the streets is marked by this, and as a voyeur to that particular misery it is hard to disentangle the shock of the indignity from the horror of her submission to it. Anne Hathaway, who plays Fantine in the 2012 movie, described sobbing 'inconsolably' in one of the most intense moments of her career as her hair was hacked off on camera. She too was paid for this, and a million strangers have watched her do it, the moment immortalised in perfect digital fidelity. When Emma Gonzales, Parkland shooting survivor, stepped in front of the world's cameras, she was both strong and tearful in a khaki jacket and a buzz cut. She became an internet icon almost immediately. Later she revealed that she'd cut her hair purely for practical reasons in the hot Florida summer. She'd had to make a PowerPoint presentation to convince her parents to let her do it.

'Language cannot do everything,' Adrienne Rich writes, and yet we are caught between this and 'a silence that strips bare'. Rich describes a moment in Carl Theodor Dreyer's 1928 silent film *The Passion of Joan of Arc* (starring Renée Jeanne Falconetti) where:

> Falconetti's face, hair shorn, a great geography
> mutely surveyed by the camera
>
> If there were a poetry where this could happen
> not as blank spaces or as words
>
> stretched like skin over meanings
> but as silence falls at the end.

Is baldness a silence, then, or a statement? Does it say something for us or about us? I have shaved my head for money. I have shaved my head for charity. I have shaved my head for someone else's sexual pleasure, though I did not know it at the time. My daughter is four years old now, fontanelle long since closed, and she wears her hair thick and long like her mama's. Like dark gold. I wonder, will I tell her this story? For as I think of it again, I find that I have to work to stretch the meaning of my dignity, like skin, over the electric tangle of circumstance, choice, intention and result beneath. Can you see it all shining there? My hair is long. My skull still feels bare.

REFERENCES

smoother than a newborn rat … Desireé Dallagiacomo (2015), 'Shave Me' from Button Poetry: www.youtube.com/watch?v=9uYTENfTO1s

biblical feminism … Sherrema Bower (2015), '"A Woman's Glory": A study exploring experiences of spiritual power and the gendered lives of women in two Pentecostal communities in the USA and New Zealand', PhD thesis: https://ourarchive.otago.ac.nz/bitstream/handle/10523/6765/BowerSherrema2015PhD.pdf ?sequence=1&isAllowed=y

Jesus, hold my earrings! … Gem Wilder (2017), 'Jesus', Turbine: http://turbinekapohau.org.nz/2017-contents-poetry-gemwilder/

a silence that strips bare … Adrienne Rich (1975), 'Cartographies of Silence': https://poetrying.wordpress.com/2008/12/15/cartographies-of-silence-adrienne-rich/

SAM KEENAN

Bad Girls

I probably would not remember Faith had she not been dead for most of my life. My recollections are slight and shadowy: a fleeting presence in her parents' house; the dark, straight curtain of her hair spilling sideways as she leaned into her younger brother's room where he was showing me a game. Faith's mother was the receptionist at my father's surgery and, very occasionally, she babysat my sisters and me. Though I only caught brief glimpses of Faith, I looked on her with the same quiet awe with which I regarded all teenagers in Westport. Teenagers wore cryptic T-shirts that said things like 'Talking Heads' and 'Simple Minds'; they yelled interesting insults like 'drop kick', 'gag me with a spoon' and 'eat shit and die'. Where I was reduced to a teary wreck in the principal's office for defying the Form 2 bus monitor, teenagers seemed capable of breaking all kinds of rules without regret.

Faith had learnt tap when she was younger, and her mother gifted me her old shoes: black leather with a clunky heel, and two round eyelets for laces on each shoe where the leather was cut into curves. In Faith's tap shoes I tapped my way to second place in a competition class that included only me. My comments sheet was returned with various suggestions for improvement from the chief judge: 'SMILE! Good girl. NO brown laces!' Faith's shoes had arrived at our house without laces, so I knew the last instruction was the fault of my parents. Faith's were the only tap shoes I owned as a child. I must have outgrown them before she died or I am sure I would have kept them, or returned them to her mother.

Westport was likely a remote kind of hell for teenagers in the 1980s. All the things that seemed important—bands, actors, fashion, concerts—the kinds of things that featured in TV annuals and *Smash Hits*—these were all somewhere else. Westport's remoteness was such that when I was six years old, a boy brought a photo of a traffic light in Christchurch to school for 'news'—a morning ritual where one presented interesting and remarkable things to other classmates. I once presented a very large spider in a jar and told the class the extraordinary fact that my father had captured it without any clothes on; another boy brought in his grandmother's freshly removed gallstones. But the traffic light—we gathered around it oohing and aahing thinking that Christchurch must be just like the movies.

When I was eleven, a year or so after my family and I had moved away from Westport, I would receive letters from my old best friend about school camp and 'pashing' and sharing sleeping bags with boys. Informed by my mother that this was disgraceful behaviour, I wrote back with faux sophistication, 'My friends here in Waikanae are far too mature to be pashing or sleeping near boys,' and our correspondence ended.

The same impulse that led my old best friend to get up to hijinks beyond her years was probably similar to the one that led Faith to hitchhiking. In the early 1980s she was known to hitch regularly from Westport to Christchurch: from Inangahua to Reefton to Culverden and over the lonely expanse known as Weka Pass, a place where bizarre rock formations emerge from green paddocks like giant sea creatures surfacing for air.

I recall very little of the day my family learned what had happened to Faith, only the hushed tones of adults, a low and muffled whispering clearly intended to exclude children from the conversation. And yet someone must have told us that Faith had died, and that this had happened because she was hitchhiking. For months there were stories about her in the *Westport News*. These were accompanied by a small black and white image of her face. I stared at Faith's photo, thinking that if I looked hard enough it would reveal something about her life story—that in a kind of palmistry, I would find the truth of what happened to her somewhere hidden within it. I thought the same about the portraits of other dead people who featured in the news—that their photos possessed some kind of extra quality that revealed they were going to die early. I worried about whether my own photos contained these terrible hidden cues, whether images of me were like the Victorian spiritualist photographs in my parents' books where a ghost passes silently in the background unbeknown to the subject, who smiles cheerfully at the camera.

Not long after Faith's death, my parents arranged for our neighbour to drive my two sisters and me to school. Our neighbour was the school dental nurse, whose laughter seemed reserved for the times in her clinic when she placed her whirring cleaning brushes against the roofs of our mouths as we tried to voice our objections through the cotton swabs stuffed into our cheeks. My memory of that morning is vivid—we pile into our neighbour's car only to have it expire five minutes into the twenty-minute journey. It splutters to a halt in a deserted place where the vast green of empty paddocks spreads uninterrupted into the distance. We exit the car and make our way up an arduously long driveway to a farmhouse bordered by black pines that make a mournful sound as the wind drifts through them. After a fruitless five minutes of knocking, we give up and return to the side of the road. Our neighbour then instructs us to put our thumbs out. I explain solemnly that we are not allowed to hitchhike and that people who hitchhike are killed.

'This is different,' our neighbour assures me. 'It is an emergency.' Her voice lingers on each syllable but I remain unconvinced. 'Your parents will understand.' Her tone is now sharp and forceful, as if she is losing patience. A truck appears in the distance. It slows as it comes closer, finally pulling over just a few metres from where we are standing. The driver, a man who looks close to the age of my father, rolls down the window and talks animatedly to our neighbour as I fidget and tremble. Our neighbour gets into the truck with the man and my sisters. I remain on the roadside fussing and procrastinating until she orders me to get in.

As I clamber inside, I notice the bright red of the vinyl interior. I do not fasten my seatbelt. Instead, I hold my hands flat and splayed out like starfish to conceal their violent shaking. I know the man is about to drive us off the main road into the depths of nowhere and murder us. The red vinyl is clearly a deliberate strategy to conceal the blood of hitchhikers. The places we pass—the cement works, Carters Beach, the flooded river churning with silt—usually so unremarkable and familiar, become dreadful and ominous. I quietly count down the moments until we are murdered. Then the truck stops. To my amazement, we have arrived at school alive and before the first bell sounds.

I never hitchhike again after that. Unlike Faith, my teenage self is neither rebellious nor brave. Instead, I define myself by sticking to rules and being supremely unadventurous. At college I studiously allocate each hour after school to learning some subject or other. My paintings in art class are defined by a hesitant impressionistic, almost pointillist style, every overlaid brushstroke having the potential to be better, more accurate, more pleasing, and (most importantly) allowing me to cover up my inevitable mistakes. I do not question the domestic laws of my family, particularly how my mother, who has two jobs, serves my father whenever he hollers 'Cup of tea!', which he does with alarming frequency.

My older sister and I experience the same punishments for transgressing boundaries. My father's preference is for a combination of sending us to our rooms and silence. If we displease him, he might refuse to speak to us for days. Being sent to one's room is an altogether different kind of discomfort. Somehow it drains every toy, every book of its attraction. I imagine how my room would appear if I did not know I was confined to it. If I chose to remain in a room and was unaware I was locked in, wouldn't I feel as if I were free to do whatever I wished, including exiting the room? Overcome by the boredom of it, I try even harder to conform.

My older sister is different. She refuses to study for exams, smokes cigarettes in her bedroom, sneaks out to meet boys, defies my father to the point of being thrown out of the house at sixteen, leaving our despairing mother to organise her accommodation and food without our father's knowledge. Because she is in a band, my older sister has ready access to all sorts of law-defying materials: cigarettes, alcohol, marijuana. She also hitchhikes.

Meanwhile, in my late teens I earnestly follow the warnings about walking home alone in the dark on the university campus, not aware of any of this affecting my freedom.

I periodically think of Faith while at this stage, but more in my twenties when I find myself in libraries with microfiches and time on my hands. I sit in the quiet of the New Zealand Room, trying to do university work but finding anything else more interesting. I flick through day after day in the *New Zealand Herald*, the *Dominion*, the *Evening Post*, becoming dizzy from the blurred screen as classifieds, sports pages and advertisements whizz past. And then I find it—Faith's death spelt out in headlines: 'Murder accused to be questioned about second body', 'Hitcher's body found stripped', 'Hitcher's death pondered', 'Rape-murder charge heard', 'Dead hitchhiker had been hit by vehicle, court told', 'Guilty of murder', 'Rape and murder lead to second life term'. As I read, I remember one of my mother's friends suggesting that the man's sentence was such that he would likely be released after six years.

One article in the *Evening Post* refers to Faith several times as a 'girl hitchhiker', calling to mind the adverts that ran on TV in the 1980s, and the bumper stickers that emphatically announced 'Girls can do anything!' When those adverts appeared back in the early eighties I remember thinking 'Everyone knows that!', despite my resolute deference to authority of which I was not yet consciously aware. The mere existence of the adverts somehow called the freedom of girls into question. More than this, what happened to Faith and the other girls who made the headlines in my youth showed me that girls could most certainly not do anything without there being dire consequences: on 1 September 1983, at around 3pm, a fourteen-year-old girl could not return from riding her horse near the Tutaekuri River in Napier; on the morning of 19 June 1987, a six-year-old girl could not get home safely after walking alone around the suburb of Maraenui in Napier; on 26 May 1989, at around 7pm, a thirteen-year-old girl could not bike back to her house from a dairy in Taita, Lower Hutt. This all cemented in my mind the importance of being unadventurous, despite the defiance that defined my childhood heroines: Anne of Green Gables, Harriet the Spy and most especially Elizabeth Allen—the lead character in Enid Blyton's book series *The Naughtiest Girl in the School*.

It's strange how the dead seem to have an afterlife in the things we discover about them, as if what we find after their deaths were part of their ongoing narrative, a posthumous action in a story that has already stopped. A friend tells me of the letter his wife hid in a book before she died, and how she knew that when he next picked it up, he'd be ready to read her words. A colleague left work suddenly after being diagnosed with a terminal illness. For weeks after her death, her out-of-office email message returned the words 'I hope to be back soon', as if sending a dispatch from wherever she now was.

In my searches for the traces of her life, I find that Faith was a postal worker, and that she was nineteen when she died. From looking through electoral rolls I discover there is a man living in Auckland who shares the same distinctive name as the man found guilty of murdering Faith. I search his name online. The man has a wife and children. When I search it again several years later he is no longer married. He has changed his job description to 'dishy'. He posts motivational messages on Facebook. He finds God. For years, there is nothing outside the paper pages of old newspapers about what he did to Faith in 1985. Then one day the internet catches up, and what he did becomes visible to the world, as if those once silent, pre-internet decades had suddenly decided to speak.

Before Faith was struck by his car, the man had earlier shot and killed a young man in Weka Pass and taken his vehicle. Faith had been making her way from Nelson to Christchurch when she was picked up by the man at Murchison. He drove her some distance and when she exited the vehicle, he ran his car into her. Hours afterwards, in the quiet fields bordering Rappahannock Road, a local panelbeater saw a newspaper blowing against a fence along with Faith's scattered possessions: books, clothing, a cardboard box, a photo album. He called the police and returned the next day with his parents to discover Faith's naked body beneath the bank by the roadside.

The articles in the *Dominion* and *Evening Post* contained scant detail on the trial, noting only that the accused claimed that he killed the young man the day before he killed Faith because 'he wouldn't leave me alone'. As for Faith, he claimed he ran into her 'by accident'. Wanting to discover more, I try to find court records, only to discover that access is restricted for 100 years after the event.

There is a 2010 song by M.I.A. called 'Bad Girls'. It begins with a half-spoken, half-sung refrain that repeats throughout the song's 348 seconds: 'Live fast, die young, bad girls do it well.' I think of Faith when I hear that song, and I think of bad as free, as boundary pushing, as defiance, as that slogan of my youth, 'Girls can do anything'. Back then I did not ask what 'anything' meant. I have vague recollections of adverts featuring women wearing hard-hats as they worked in construction sites, presumably to show that women could work in traditionally male-dominated vocations. But what about existing in the world? Could that same woman walk alone through her own workplace at night without feeling fearful? If she was there after 10pm and someone harmed her, would she be met with the question 'What were you doing there?', as if her choice to be somewhere in the world at a certain time made her in some way stupid, or careless, or partially responsible, as if she could have foreseen what would happen to her, and all she had to do to avoid it was to not be out alone late at night for the rest of her life?

I am still waiting to be brave like Faith, to be someone who more openly takes on 'the rules'. On particularly long stretches of road, the kind where the scenery is almost luminously green and leads into a personless wilderness, I sometimes imagine I see her—her posture giving away her fierce independence, her hair lifted by the wind, her bag slung on her shoulders as she walks with her thumb out, full of anticipation for her next trip to the city, emphatically doing the 'Anything' we eighties girls were told we could. My mother remembers hearing Faith's favourite song at her funeral: 'Turn, Turn, Turn' by the Byrds. More particularly, she remembers being upset at its suggestion of the inevitability of the events in life, as if there is set out before us 'a time to every purpose under heaven'.

Almost thirty years after her death I visit Faith's grave in the Orowaiti Cemetery on Utopia Road just outside of Westport. From the small hillocks you can see the estuary where land, river and sea intermingle. In heavy rain the cemetery has been known to flood, leaving only the headstones visible, rising vertically from the surface as if straining to keep themselves above water. On Faith's grave there is a quotation from 'Burnt Norton', the first poem of T.S. Eliot's *Four Quartets*:

> Footfalls echo in the memory
> Down the passage which we did not take
> Towards the door we never opened
> Into the rose-garden.

I lay down a bunch of pink carnations, wishing I had brought roses instead. I look over the fields where a light wind makes small waves of the overgrown grass that obscures the Victorian graves in the older part of the cemetery. For several minutes I watch the patterns, the rhythmic bend of the blades, thinking of Faith and the other girls who made the newspapers in my youth, the strange and unknowable unopened doors of their once-possible futures. I look around to see if I am still alone. I take a deep breath. I look around again, then I leave.

TOBY BUCK

Aquae Populus
A profile of a rural community sauna

The picture is not complete without some quarrelsome fellow, a thief caught in the act, or the man who loves the sound of his own voice in the bath—not to mention those who jump in with a tremendous splash. —SENECA, First Century AD

Things have been heading south with Warren for some time.

We don't agree on sauna politics. And we don't agree on politics, so things are getting awkward. That we are adults sitting in our togs, sweating profusely, just makes things worse.

Why sauna? Do you go? Over winter I visit my local sauna to escape the cold. For me, that means relaxed silence. When I can get it, it's true luxury. But for Warren, sauna time is different. I suspect Warren goes to the sauna just to talk.

Also, side note, Warren likes to talk.

It's met with a lot of eye-rolling from other people there, also in their togs. Warren's stories are beratingly 'big', and often centre on 'the way things really are' or 'what you should all know about this'.

I wish I didn't find Warren's company or conversation style tough going. But there are layers to this. I've been coming here for over two years and, even if I did want to talk, any exchange with Warren is barely a conversation. It's a one-way, hard-line, right-leaning rant. I'm no fan. But, really, it's the bravado that's the most overbearing. The big-necked, chest-puffed-up-ness of the proclamations. The knee-jerk righteousness with a veil-of-unquestionability thrown over it. No one else gets a right of reply. For anyone listening it's tough, tough going.

Warren likes to sit with his head in his hands, then look up suddenly and say something. Or, he'll stand, turn and put one leg up on the wooden sauna seat, shake his head slightly and stare philosophically into the middle distance before making a pronouncement. An odd choice when the only visible middle distance is the lane instructions on the door to the swimming pool. Someone's scratched out the L on the lettering, so for the past year it's read 'Please swim in a c ockwise fashion.'

But that's Warren. A dramatic talker.

I have learnt from Warren:

1. He is very into property. In a big way.
2. He was, in his youth, an agile and dangerous martial arts practitioner and is not here to make friends.
3. He's here to stay in shape.
4. He is more than comfortable sincerely using the phrase 'fake news'.

I have indirectly learnt from Warren that:

1. Some deal went bad once.
2. He has grudges. 'Some people? Urgh. Just. Some people. Ammiright?'
3. He has grievances. 'Grumble grumble. Grumble, grumble grumble.'

Across cultures hot springs have been places of therapy for millennia. All public bathing shares this ancient heritage and tradition: a common space, usually secular, for physical relaxation, interaction and some sociability. New Zealand may not be ancient Rome, but with all the natural geothermal activity here (there are over a hundred accessible thermal springs) gathering socially to swim and warm ourselves is part of our cultural history. It would be hubristic to presume even the small local sauna I attend is somehow apart from that tradition.

Although the social rules are subtle, the sauna functions as a psychological pressure valve for the town. The swell of people, opportunity and custom over the summer months is followed here by cold, dark winters with few healthy and inexpensive leisure options. Amusement is a self-made thing over the colder months, and the sauna—as well as being a place of literal warmth—functions as a gentle antidote to the somewhat remorseless seasonality of rural life. The temporary casual integration it offers is apposite to the disconnection people can feel here.

Plus, you know. It's warm.

The sauna is in a small gym complex on the western edge of town—between the row of McDonald's, Burger King and KFC known as 'fast-food alley' and the road out, away from the coast. It's the most industrial part of town, selling farm equipment, horse-riding gear, work uniforms with steel-cap boots.

The gym buildings are run by Florian and his wife, whom no one's met. Florian's in his early forties and, decked out in his bright red puffer jacket and often holding a plastic bag of snack food, usually stands at the reception where the gym connects to the sauna and four-lane pool.

There are raffle tickets to win a meat pack that includes a size 14 chicken. Proceeds to get a defibrillator onsite. A whiteboard sign asks parents of kids taking swimming classes to make sure they're paid for in advance. A big plastic tub by the door holds lost property: hoodies, jandals, towels, kids' clothes and bright plastic water bottles. There's a notice taped to the counter reminding people about the open-water swim this weekend off the harbour point, by the new subdivision.

As gyms go, the place is far from the world of mirror-watching workouts, Lycra and spin classes. It's a community gym, tucked between the physical rehab centre and the city hospital.

Repairs to the building have been running behind for years. The occasional light flickers, the odd tile is cracked, but no one who uses the place seems too concerned. There's a weights room, a few treadmills, and two taiaha next to the yoga mats in case you want to practise for kapa kaka.

The Mongrel Mob has headquarters nearby. A few younger patched-up members come in to work out, plus an older crew with gang tattoos but a more solid and easy-going bearing.

Training for the Iron Māori competition is 6am on Tuesdays and Thursdays, and men and women pour into the small sauna after with a chorus of 'Mōrena' and 'Pomare e.' As each woman enters the men shuffle about to give her the best seat, making a tiny bit of a show about it. Tattoos are common here too. And either a 'G'day everyone' or a round of 'Chur chur' with an upward nod is expected any time of day you come in.

Busy before work and after, the sauna holds about twelve at the most. The closeness makes it a degree more intimate. If someone else is there when you are, it would feel slightly oppressive to sit in complete silence without acknowledging their presence. It's necessary to interact a little. But, on the flipside, the garrulous are unavoidable. When it's full the sauna's more social than a swimming pool. Each day the sauna regulars take up their favourite spots on the wooden benches. The volume is more like a bar than a café.

There's a bottle of water you spritz on the element to raise humidity, and a fifteen-minute timer on the wall you're supposed to flip over when you do.

*

When the pool opens at 6am the first into the sauna are four women in their sixties. They sauna before and after they've aqua-jogged. They're very chatty and, when in the pool, are constantly trying to avoid getting their hair wet. They're nice to everyone but they greatly, and vocally, prefer swimmers who don't dive in or splash about.

One other lady, slightly younger, has Tourette's and aqua-jogs a metre or two behind the group talking to herself. Her half-hearted, softly repeated words are an echo-like riff of what she catches from the conversation of the other four.

Towels under their arms, the first men into the sauna at that time of the day are Tony and Marty.

Tony is a former teacher in his seventies who catches whitebait and knows every local fishing spot and how to access it. Every season is different for whitebait, and favourite sites coveted and fought over. Conversation with Tony is serious and endlessly varied as long as you enjoy talking about whitebait.

He's sharp and convivial and has nicknames for everyone. Not all nice. Tony's known for being a bit on the sharp side of sharp. Too sharp for some people.

He collected postage stamps for years and now sells them at the Sunday market in Napier. He gives away sets to people if he thinks they'll be appreciated. He's a proponent of colloidal silver and considers diluted peroxide in your drinking water a panacea. He used to advocate hard for both theories but now he waves it off.

'Just Google it. All the facts are there.'

Tony's innately gifted with the serial-monologist's knack of deriving complete satisfaction from his own conversation, without requiring any external participation. He alternates his fishing diatribes with a needling of other sauna users for his own sly entertainment.

Tony also likes to talk when getting changed. This is a subset of sauna user—the type who likes to continue the conversation seamlessly in the changing rooms, often standing naked, showering or towelling off while still holding forth. If the image that comes to the reader's mind is graphic I apologise and can only offer that, in person, the experience is at least as worrying.

Tony is married, and his number is taped to my fridge in case I want to go fishing sometime. Tony and I on the ocean. On a small boat. I am. Still. Undecided.

Marty, who's usually in there with Tony, is a former jockey in his sixties whose kids are all in Australia. There are a few jockeys who use the sauna to 'lose those last few pounds'. He cycles to the sauna each day in his bright yellow Hi-Viz even after two bouts of knee surgery, which he doesn't like to talk about. He waves if you see him on the road turning in.

Quieter, more charitable, but also gruffer and a bit sweary, Marty's a natural offsider to Tony and likes to keep things to the point. He proudly has 'no patience for bloody fools'. I keep thinking he'd be great in a Harry Potter story except I know he'd keep going off-script. 'Jeez, Harry, stop waving your wand about, you bloody ponce! Pull your damn finger out and get on with it. Or just shut your bloody mouth for five minutes.'

Around midday Dave arrives and is immediately superb, life-of-the-party-type company. He's Māori, mid-forties and very restless. A constant mover. A few times Dave's introduced himself as 'Dave the Māori'—which he finds funnier than anyone else. He works in forestry and is always stretching, walking and stalking, rolling his head around his neck and shoulders. He switches places with people perching by the door and stands and opens it to let the next person in.

Dave's part of a crew that accesses parts of inland forest two hours from town, where they'll be stationed for days, rising before daybreak on cold winter mornings to drive further inland as needed.

He usually has a big Bluetooth speaker set to highest volume in the changing room next door, so everyone has to listen. He plays a blend of Motown, 1980s hip hop and disco. I love it. However, it is apparently popular among only about half the sauna folk.

Whenever it comes up in conversation Dave grins.

'Well, anyone who doesn't like it can always go fuck themselves.'

Little-known Dave facts:

1. Dave's daughter was a recent Miss New Zealand.
2. Dave has a 1959 Chevrolet Impala in storage.

Dave is cagey about me knowing about his beautiful muscle car. But he's told me he takes it out in the Spring Parade and the Street Art Festival each March. Once he turned up in a black and white gangster pinstripe, hat and spats included, and said he was taking the car out for a Sunday drive. Diplomatic and social, Dave's far too smart and fast moving to be caught in any arguments.

Mid-afternoon is usually when Alan and Gus arrive. Father and son, they only talk sport, and Alan is particularly sagacious. He moves slowly, always careful not to cause offence with his comments. Gus is closer to my age and once told me about his previous P addiction, and how he'd moved on to smoking. And about his ex. 'Total bitch.' I think he has a kid. There's something acrimonious ongoing but it's hard to get a handle on the details.

They come in the same car, have the same tall and lean build and look like twins aged thirty years apart. They seem to agree with everyone about most things but since they only talk about league or basketball it's a bit hard to tell.

Sandy is in about 5pm. She runs a hostel for long-term tenants and talks mostly about the guests' behaviour and her latest boyfriend. If people don't engage she'll complain loudly: 'The reason I like this gym is because it's not full of stuck-up white people! People here talk!'

Everyone usually chuckles awkwardly. There are very few possible responses that don't sound forced. If you guessed the response to be 'Hey Sandy, how's your boyfriend?' then you are 100 per cent correct.

Sandy will happily furnish more detail than anyone requires.

'I've only seen him on Monday and Wednesday this week. But wow, it's so physical! He just won't stop. Nothing like my last boyfriend. Really! Unstoppable!'

There's usually some unsettled throat-clearing and everyone tries to look elsewhere. Difficult in a small room, when the air suddenly seems a little closer and a little hotter than before.

It's easy to be negative about Sandy. She complains a lot about her tenants and their life choices, she's pugnacious and leans forward into every topic, and just loves having the last word. There's a rumour she's from 'old money'.

'Seriously well off.' But it's worth mentioning that she's also incredibly generous and sincere. She's constantly lending people things, and a member of the Hastings DIY Coffin Club as well.

As the name suggests, this group gets together weekly to build their own coffins. There's nothing religious about it, and it's as sociable as a bridge or tennis club. Building your own coffin is practical and cheap. Some coffins are very plain but others are painted bright colours, bedazzled and upholstered with patterns from Spotlight. Coffins lean up against the front of the house where the club meets, looking like something between a garage sale and the village undertaker's in a country and western film.

I have a hundred questions about this and want to join, but it's pretty much a closed group.

Sandy also regularly replaces the plastic flowers at the Mary of the Crossroads just out of town. She helps tidy the graves in the chapel cemetery there. For years local families have decorated them with artificial flowers, coloured ribbons and bright plastic toy windmills positioned to catch the breeze.

*

In a sauna everyone's prone to some degree of self-consciousness. It's like the sideline at a Saturday sports game except for the fact that we're sitting here almost in our underwear. This lends an extra layer of intimacy to the social experience. Some people become confessional, or flirtatious, some are performative and others shy and determinedly anonymous.

Generally, sauna conversation works around a few key themes. Land is one. Water another. Grape growers are happy when it's dry in summer, farmers when there's some rain. Local water being bottled and sold for supposedly vast profit offshore is a sore point. The proposed dam another.

When Marcus, a cattle farmer from the back country, comes in, he's self-deprecating and even tempered. He's cautious with his opinion on summer water shortages, especially since inland Bay farmers are expected to benefit from upcoming plans. He doesn't even rise to Warren calling his home town all 'sheep shit and electric fences'.

The pub there closed recently. There wasn't the population to support it. It was bought by a pair of local farming brothers who had been throwing big drinking parties there. But it's no good for taking a date, so Marcus drives forty minutes to pick up his girlfriend from Napier and bring her to the sauna to relax. After, he says, they like to go to 'that Turkish place for some goss, a cuddle, and a Chicken Iskender'.

Current sauna talk is mostly about a winery putting a new walking track up the face of the local peak.

'It's their land. They paid for it.'

'Whose land first? There's Māori bones everywhere up there. No-go spots.'

'The land's private.'

'But everyone has to see it and the owners don't even live here!'

'People are rubbish.'

'Especially people spending taxpayer money.'

A popular and perennial hero is Inky, the squid who escaped last year from the New Zealand National Aquarium. There was an article in *The New York Times*: 'Inky the Escapee Octopus'. In the sauna there's civic pride about the ingenuity of our own cephalopod-made-good.

'Undid his tank after seeing staff do it. Hauled himself eight feet over the lino to a 164-foot-long drainpipe. Then "plop". Into the sea. Off to see a lady. Bloody legend.'

There's a similar running joke about Manukura—the white kiwi at the Pukaha Wildlife Centre. He's known for being unable to stop himself chasing the females around in his aviary. To the innocent delight of children and the more arch amusement of parents.

With sauna talk it's sometimes hard to tell exactly when a subject is done. There's a sense of everything being a bit unresolved. Subjects like Inky, or water shortages, get batted about as long as people care to keep chipping in. There's a strong urge to keep any good joke or fruitful topic going. Tony or Warren will make a statement, there'll be silence for ten minutes, then the same subject will be restarted, with new sauna entrants providing an audience to be canvassed afresh.

Enabling this is a steady run of backpackers, school kids, retirees, tourists, out-patients from the hospital and one-time visiting locals. A small busload of Japanese tourists one Friday morning seemed to arrive by mistake. They were as gregarious and social as anyone and, as far as people could understand, also on the lookout for John Kirwan.

French and Italian backpackers here to pick blueberries mix with meat workers from the freezing works and talk about unions and hourly rates. As nationalities attempt to find common ground there's an unconscious tendency to imitate in gesture, then language. Tony, who points this out to me, says it's called echopraxia and echolalia.

Sinta from Indonesia works on orchards, doesn't speak much English, and is mostly on his phone texting or making calls. He wants to take his kids and wife back home to visit Jakarta for three weeks at Christmas. But it's not cheap and Sinta is working weekends to make it happen.

He manages a crew of 150 seasonal workers from the Pacific—mostly Vanuatu, Marlborough and the East Cape this year. His company provides work for up to nine months of the year for some sorting recruitment, bank accounts, accommodation, health and safety, and daily work. They usually fill the local exercise classes on Tuesday and Thursday at 5.30pm. After a day of picking, pruning or packing they arrive in the three full white minivans to box, jog, cycle and stretch. People want to talk about the cyclones that hit Vanuatu and here on the East Cape this year. But almost all conversation is limited to grins, nods and thumbs up. On the first day of winter they withdraw months of pay in cash before flying home *en masse*.

Among the one-off visitors this summer was the Kiwi mixed martial arts fighter living on the Gold Coast, who kept shaving and moisturising himself. Also a young guy drinking Woodstock & Cola who popped out then came back in naked, explaining he was trying to fit in a quick drink and a workout before he met his probation officer. The logic of his plan eluded us all.

Most conversational gambits are met with a fair amount of generosity and tolerance. From a purely practical point of view, choosing when to disagree with someone in a confined space, and how much, must be done strategically.

There's a guy whose name I've never known. Looks like a grumpy Van Morrison. Shaved head. Speaks in short sentences. He has a white spotted pitbull he brings to the pool that runs alongside his lane as he swims. He stops at each end, pausing to rub the dog's ears and tell it not to jump in.

Afterwards, in the sauna, he's terse and tense, and his stories, as soon as he knows you're listening, are extreme. He speaks only one-on-one. If there's a crowd, he's silent. One, two, three car accident tales in quick succession. Then the time he pulled a man out of a burning truck when he heard a bang outside the pub.

'Went back after and finished my pint!'

I was suspicious of that one.

But he did say he could barely drink it since his whole body was shaking with adrenaline. He seemed so full of adrenaline telling the story the sauna seemed too small a room to question it. Though dissenting in close quarters might cross your mind, this is usually outweighed by a more egalitarian need to simply interact and allow someone to be, even momentarily, heard.

The sauna's social ecosystem tends to self-correct to its own even keel.

*

While the people who use this place, and the ways they use it, are distinct, contemporary and varied, the patterns of interaction are the same as millennia ago. It's not a manicured or homogenised experience. It's endlessly irregular. The carousel of local archetypes, plus the retinue of visitors, echo age-old tropes. The sport, practicalities and jostling for position in conversation seem as timeless and ageless as the irrepressible human urge to communicate.

Last week, however, there was a notice in the paper. Florian and his wife are moving on. So for now the gym and sauna are, at least temporarily, closed.

A few instructors are out of work, and kids' swimming classes have been cancelled. The notice says the owners have advised anyone making automatic payments to stop. Posted on the gym's Facebook page is the message 'Thank you all—it has been a blast and a privilege!'

The last time I went to the sauna, an Italian visitor spent thirty minutes explaining that the most similar place to Italy he'd been in New Zealand was the carpark outside PAK'nSAVE in Hastings.

I realise I haven't seen Warren in more than a month.

Of all the sauna patrons, Warren was the only one 100 per cent committed to using his line of conversation like a hammer. I'd never contributed or encouraged. But I'd been present for the speeches and watched unsuspecting visitors slowly realise what they've walked into and why everyone else in the sauna is silent.

'What New Zealand needs is a Donald Trump!' Warren had declared. 'A real businessman who knows how to take charge!'

This was the only occasion I dared respond, saying mildly that I wasn't so sure. Personally. Since then Warren and I haven't spoken.

The only time he addressed me directly was after he'd martialled court so successfully that I was the only one left in the room. And I wasn't responding. He leaned in conspiratorially as he was leaving.

'I talk too much. I know. You don't. I get it. You're quiet. But it's okay. Everyone's different here. People like me just like to talk.'

Which is a fair summation.

And what would I know?

I should also report that Warren has bad knees and must clamber about carefully. And that after the sauna he likes to jump feet first into the deep end of the swimming pool with a tremendous splash. And that he combs his hair for a very long time. And that, for all that noise, he is himself quite quiet and shy outside of the sauna.

REFERENCES

The picture is not complete … Quote displayed on a pillar at the Roman baths at Aqua Sulis in Somerset. Anna Lydia Motto, *Seneca's Epistles* (Mundelein, Illinois: Bolchazy-Carducci Publishers, 2001).

New Zealand may not be ancient Rome … Sally Jackson, *Hot Springs of New Zealand Guide Book* (4th Edition) (Hot Water Publishing, 2017).

One Eye Open

You have twelve cranial nerves. You probably didn't know that. Why should you? Unless you're a doctor—or someone like me—you probably also haven't given much thought to the fact that the seventh of these travels through a narrow canal of bone beneath the ear to the nerves of the face. That if the nerve gets inflamed and swells, signals stop going through, like water through the hose you stepped on one summer. That it just so happens those signals allow you to do things you take for granted every day: whistle a tune while you wash the dishes, blow up balloons for your son's sixth birthday party, smile broadly when your young daughter gives you a card she's made from construction paper and covered with heart stickers. If you're someone like me, who can't do these things, cranial nerves—how many and what they do—take on a new interest. What I would give to whistle. What I'd give for my face to look the way it used to. Not like Brad Pitt's or anything. Just normal. Like yours.

Like so many stories, this one began with a clue too subtle for notice: a headache on a Wednesday in late April 2012. To that point, it had been a normal year. We'd planted pumpkins behind our home at the time, in the village of Ashhurst outside Palmerston North. I'd just published my second book of poetry, *A History of Glass*, and had arranged some readings in the US for May. I spent a good number of hours from Wednesday to Friday that week on the phone with airlines, trying to find a way to get my family to the US on air points. The process was frustrating and stressful. As I'm prone to stress headaches, I didn't pay this one particular mind. I just popped some paracetamol. I did notice the headache didn't respond; that the pain focused, unusually, on the right side of my head; that it seemed to be getting worse. I took a bite of my sandwich on the Thursday and it tasted terrible: I'd lost taste on the right side of my tongue. By Friday, the headache had migrated clearly to my right ear. I assumed I had an ear infection. The doctor's schedule was full, so

I resolved to see how it felt in the morning and to go to urgent care if it hadn't improved. I went to bed Friday night with a blazing earache. Saturday morning I woke up with half a face.

Maybe you wonder why I'm telling you this. For sympathy? Hardly. Look at the news. Refugees. Kids separated from parents. Countries going under the sea. If you have anything left in your emotional transaction account, this is hardly the place to spend it. And still, oddly, I go on talking.

Maybe, like me, you've misread the clue that had finally announced itself as one. Like many people who wake up unable to smile and with trouble closing one eye, I assumed I was having a stroke. My wife put me in the car, piled in the kids and took me to A&E (she had her doubts about a stroke, as I was offering helpful suggestions on her driving). I sat in the waiting room impatiently. I kept asking the nurse behind the window for aspirin. If I'm having a stroke, I said, shouldn't I be getting some aspirin? Why won't anyone give me some goddamn aspirin? When I finally saw the doctor, he explained that they first need a brain scan—an aspirin would make a potential bleed in the brain a lot worse. So much for knowing everything. A CT scan operator had to be called in from home to get a picture of my brain. Did I have a stroke or not? I asked when the doctor finally appeared with the results. 'Nothing that exciting,' he said. He handed me an information sheet on Bell's Palsy.

From the outside, if you knew me then, it looked simply as if my face had stopped working. It was a bit more complicated from the inside. Two days later I couldn't close my right eye at all, so I had to frequently apply ointment and drops, and use tape the eye to keep it shut at night so it didn't dry out. The facial paralysis was accompanied by headaches, earaches, dizziness, hyperacusis (everything seemed unpleasantly loud), and—for a frightening couple of days— neuralgia, a nerve pain that is agonising and debilitating: little zaps of lightning through my neck and chest so that all I could do was sit in bed and try not to move.

Though I was desperate for information, it was hard to read the computer for any length of time. My cursory searching online indicated that 85 per cent of Bell's Palsy patients make significant recovery within three weeks; 71 per cent eventually recover full function. To give a sense of how clearly I was thinking, I said we should go ahead and host a planned dinner party the next weekend with several other couples. My wife took a firm hand, persuading me that this was absurd. Still, I clung to the information that a substantial recovery was possible in under three weeks.

Before my face collapsed, I had succeeded in getting plane tickets to the US. My first reading, in Baltimore, was almost exactly three weeks away. My wife stepped in again and said we should consider cancelling our trip, but this time I demurred. The timing was perfect. I should be in pretty good shape by then to read some poems to a crowd. As they say on the beer ads: *Yeah, right.*

This has nothing to do with you, right? Yet you probably know someone who's had Bell's Palsy, and I hate to say it but the odds you'll get it are shorter than you think. An old friend in the US who saw me at my worst—we hadn't been in contact for a long time—waved her hand without concern: *Yeah,* she said, *I had that.* The incidence of Bell's Palsy, depending on where you get your information, is between 11 and 40 per 100,000 people each year. To look at it another way, an annual rate of 20 people per 100,000—one cited rate in the literature—means that one out of 60 people will get it over a lifetime.

*

Bell's Palsy is a diagnosis of exclusion. Facial palsy has been linked as a symptom to, among other things, sarcoidosis, Lyme disease, diabetes, brain tumours and multiple sclerosis. Once these causes are reasonably ruled out, the problem is attributed to Bell's Palsy. So why, then, does the facial palsy occur? You have to keep asking that question to get to the central ignorance around this ailment. It happens because the seventh cranial nerve becomes inflamed, blocking signals. Why does the nerve become inflamed? At various times the blame has been laid, according to an article in the *Western Journal of Medicine*, on 'viral infection, vascular ischemia, autoimmune inflammatory disorders, and heredity'. The viral theory is the most widely accepted. Testing suggests that many cases are the result of the reactivation of some remnant of the oral herpes simplex virus (HSV-1). That's a cold sore virus that most of us (probably you) happen to carry, dormant, on nerve tissues. (This is not the same as HSV-2, the genital herpes virus.) The facial nerve swells in reaction to the virus, cutting off signals to the muscles. Why does the dormant virus get reactivated? No one knows. Stress, illness, trauma, bad karma. I had a flu shot the Wednesday the symptoms started, which made me suspicious, but studies have refuted any connection. Charles Bell first described it nearly 200 years ago. And still we don't know.

As there is a 1 in 60 chance you will find yourself at A&E in this sort of predicament, it might be good to know to ask for two medications typically given to Bell's Palsy patients. One is prednisone, a steroid. The other is an antiviral such as acyclovir. As an article in *American Family Physician* put it: 'Approximately 70 to 80 percent of patients will recover spontaneously; however, treatment with a seven-day course of acyclovir or valacyclovir and a tapering course of prednisone, initiated within three days of the onset of symptoms, is recommended to reduce the time to full recovery and increase the likelihood of complete recuperation.'

However, this treatment course is not wholly accepted. Studies tend to support prednisone, though not with complete confidence, and tend to cast more doubt on acyclovir. Still, I recommend you get both. I was given only the prednisone by the A&E registrar (when he found out I was lecturer, he looked a little worried and said, not quite joking, 'I hope not of medicine'). I didn't get the acyclovir until I had a follow-up with my general practitioner a week later and by then it was probably too late; he was annoyed that A&E hadn't prescribed it. Prednisone made me (even more) prone to outbursts of anger. And because I could only move part of my mouth, I had trouble articulating my words, getting people to understand me. I'd call a shop about something. *What?* they'd ask. *Can you repeat that name?* Whatever my other failings, until then I was always able to communicate. The combination of the prednisone, my frustration and the pain was a potent one. After one difficult phone call I slammed my laptop shut in such frustration that I destroyed the hard drive. I'm writing this on its successor.

You will perhaps not be surprised, as I was, that my face showed no sign of recovery by the day of my reading in the US three weeks later. My body had no interest in my professional timetable, nor in the optimistic recovery statistics. At some point in the first month my hearing returned to normal. But along with ongoing complete paralysis on the right side of my face, the loss of taste continued, as did the headache, earache and a strange lightheadedness that became for months and months a daily companion, giving the world a kind of distance.

The readings were a farce, of course, though everyone pretended otherwise. Family and friends came to the Ivy Bookshop in Baltimore, some from as far as New York. Half my face wasn't working. I could barely articulate my name. But I stubbornly stood there and read poems for half an hour. I made a joke of it. 'And now a poem as read by Sylvester Stallone.' People were kind. They laughed. They bought the book.

The fact is, I was impatient with illness. I wanted it gone. I wanted to be myself, to be seen as myself. I had taken to wearing a pirate-style patch over my right eye to protect it from dirt, dust, leaves, inadvertent pokes by my young son (I had no protective blink reflex). While in Baltimore, wearing the patch, I dropped by a friend's house with some of the other old friends in town. We fell into the old playful rhythms and it was the most normal I'd felt for a long time. There was a parrot in the house. One of my friends put it on my shoulder and took a photo.

I returned to my teaching job a month or so after my diagnosis, declining my department head's offer for more time off. I was oddly worried that it would in some way put my job at risk. It was a heavy teaching year. We were moving to a new building in August, which required sorting through eight years of files, packing boxes. I was coordinator for our English programme.

I was sleeping hours later than usual whenever I could—I used to wake easily at 6:30, but now my wife let me sleep quite late on weekends, so she bore the brunt of the kids' early rising. I still couldn't move the right side of my face. I was in pain and dizzy, constantly exhausted. Still, I kept it all going. I was in a hurry to get better and to be seen that way.

Needless to say, I wasn't at my best that year as a teacher. I forgot meetings. As English coordinator I barely held it together. But I pretended I was well enough to carry on, and eventually people started to believe me. I took occasional short-cuts. To make my life easier I scheduled a writing workshop at a time that, as I found out later, conflicted with a colleague's class. There were a couple of other options on the timetable but they would have vastly complicated my life, made things much harder. The overlap affected four students. When I declined my colleague's request to shift the workshop she yelled at me with such vehemence and contempt I was uncharacteristically speechless. But why shouldn't she spit her ire at me? I was fully recovered, wasn't I?

Domestic life continued in our semi-rural home. After a bumper crop of
pumpkins we watched the vines dwindle until they nearly disappeared. We
popped the misshapen bells from the vines, even the ones grown the wrong
way over the fence into the neighbour's paddock, and piled them on the porch;
we planted lettuce, beetroot, carrots. The whole garden had a kind of tired,
morning-after wrinkle, a bed left unmade by someone headed for the hospital
half dressed. An inflamed nerve pressing bone, no signals running through
the wire. A face sort of leaning down and to the right. What's a face? Only who
you've been. My wife did all the digging, shooed me to the couch, the hens to
their run. A matter of waiting: would the lettuces survive the frost, beetroot
grow, broccoli flower, chickens return to the lay, pumpkins self-seed to rise next
season from shrivelled vines to the fullness of former selves? Nothing to do all
winter but let time take its time. Two months, then three. The world half-frozen.
I offered it half a grin. My wife, mulching rows with priestly patience, searched
for signs of life. Shopkeepers treated me too kindly, like maybe I was an idiot.
Anything seemed possible. I kept one eye open.

At this stage in any drama, you will expect some good news, then a reversal,
and I will not disappoint. My right upper lip started to move slightly in July.
Gradually I saw more improvement over the next few months. I could eat
without biting my lip. I could with some effort partly move the right side of
my mouth. Most importantly, by October I could close my right eye (no more
swimming goggles in the shower to keep shampoo out of my eye). I had a blink
reflex, too. Finally, after six months, I thought I was home free. But then the
improvement slowed. A new problem emerged. Essentially, the nerves had
been paralysed for so long that when they came back to life they mis-wired.
This condition, called synkinesis, is common for slow healers, for those with
particularly deep palsies. When I closed my eye, the right side of my mouth
visibly pulled upwards and vice versa—when I smiled, my right eye closed.
When I ate, my eye watered: you can still tell I've enjoyed a meal because tears
stream down the right side of my face. My right eye became noticeably smaller
than the left. During the worst of the facial palsy the right side of my face had
drooped, as if I were the stroke victim I'd thought I was. Now, as though my
body had worked too hard to correct the problem, the synkinesis pulled the
right side of my mouth oddly upwards against gravity. I gave a lecture in this

new condition. There was no normal connection with the students, no energy in the room, no response to my efforts at humour. They just gaped. Just as things seemed to be improving, I looked again like a freak.

Enter a sort of saviour. I was meant to present at a conference in Boston in March 2013, so I scheduled a stop to see family in Baltimore. My wife suggested that I investigate whether there were any Bell's Palsy experts at Johns Hopkins Hospital. I did and there was. I emailed him, a plastic surgeon and ear, nose and throat specialist (it turned out his wife is from New Zealand). He agreed to see me. I showed up at his office on 28 February and within minutes of examining me he recommended outpatient neck surgery. He planned to cut some of the platysma muscle to release my face and reduce a lot of the tension that was causing the right side to pull upwards. It was Thursday, and I was leaving for Boston the following Tuesday. This was a man who had patients coming to him from all over the world. Nevertheless, the next day he was cutting my throat.

The surgery made an immediate difference. I left his office with a face that looked abnormal but much more relaxed. Thirty units of Botox also helped my appearance (temporarily). My Hopkins doctor—to whom I am incredibly grateful—referred me to a physical therapist who showed me a series of facial exercises. For example, I had to say certain phrases and try to prevent my eye from closing while I talked. Three times a day for at least seven weeks I had to give myself visual feedback to retrain my face to act normally. F, V, B, M—these letters in particular tended to cause my eye to close, to flutter heavily. *Feed farmer Fred* I'd say over and over to the face in the mirror. *A victory for Victor. Make Mary's mother more milk.* Eventually I could talk without my eye fully closing at every second word, though even now when I'm tired or anxious— sometimes speaking to a new acquaintance—it returns.

Meanwhile, other symptoms started to worry me. In addition to the headaches and earaches, my hands trembled. The vision in my right eye was blurring, making it harder to read the computer. I had tingling in my chin. At various times I was certain the facial palsy was some indictor of a deeper neurological problem. Given that Bell's Palsy is a diagnosis of exclusion, this wasn't completely out of the realm of possibility, and the internet loves to feed on medical ambiguity. On Monday I was sure I had MS. By Wednesday I was certain I had early signs of Parkinson's. A week later I was convinced I had an acoustic neuroma.

These symptoms continued for another eighteen months. Finally I asked my GP to refer me to a private neurologist, accessible because I had private insurance, something I'd not thought to use earlier. The neurologist did a thorough assessment. Nothing wrong with you, he said. To be conservative, he arranged an MRI (but only after a wait of six weeks during which I had to stay off paracetamol and ibuprofen—'the junk,' he called it—to ensure I wasn't suffering rebound headaches). The MRI result was negative. Before I left his office, in Wellington, he dictated his notes in front of me. 'Dr Walpert,' he said, 'is still getting accustomed to his new disability.' My GP put it more bluntly: aside from the obvious—residual facial paralysis, synkinesis, related pain—my only problem was anxiety. 'The new Bryan is different from the old Bryan,' he said. 'You've had a shock to the system.'

If you're like most people, you'll pretend when you see me that you don't notice the distortion in my face. Or maybe you'll be kind and tell me I don't look that different, or even that I'm looking better. I appreciate it—I have improved a bit—but there is no getting around reality. Kids routinely ask about my face. On a family trip to the US my son got teased on the playground about my eye: the boy asked my son if New Zealand was an alien planet. A New Zealand poet, a woman I hadn't seen in five years, touched my hand, looked me in the eye, and said, 'I'm not saying you're not now, but you *were* a very good-looking young man.'

Do you think I don't know there are many ailments far worse than Bell's Palsy? I am otherwise, as my GP put it without irony, 'a picture of health'. I thought about his use of 'picture'. How important are our faces? According to a 2011 article in *Philosophical Transactions of the Royal Society B*: '[H]umans readily draw a number of conclusions about the personality attributes, appearance, emotional states and preferences of complete strangers solely on the basis of facial cues.' I don't know whether to mention the history of my face to someone I haven't seen in years, or whether to let it go—for their sake or mine. I avoid photographs and, if I can't, try not to smile. Facebook? Think about the very name of that site—not sure I'm the target audience. People post photos of me sometimes and I cringe. I try to get used to the fact that I don't look quite like myself any more, that some people react to me differently—I can see the hesitation, the unspoken query.

And I wait to see whether the whole thing will strike again. Though one in 60–70 people will get Bell's Palsy over the course of their lives, roughly one in 14 of those who have had Bell's Palsy will get it again, either on the same side or on the other.

I started out in a hurry to get better. Seven years after losing my face, I am in limbo. I'm not sick, but I'm not who I was. A counsellor encourages acceptance: 'But how is the new Bryan the *same* as the old Bryan?' My Johns Hopkins doctor suggests a fairly substantial facial reanimation surgery that would require transferring a muscle from my leg to my face. But I worry I will end up simply another not-me, just different from the current not-me. Accept or refuse. Resist or embrace. What would you do?

*

And why on earth am I telling you all of this? I think it's because Bell's Palsy is, in the grand scheme of things, a nothing that feels nevertheless like a something. I think it's because I hate an elephant in a room, so I'm the one who points at it. I think it's because I'm invisible and want to be seen again. Me, I mean: the guy behind the face. What better than this? We're equals here. No videos, no photos. Just old school—words on a page. Here you don't have to acknowledge what I look like or tell me I look fine.

Still, it's hard to hide behind the page forever. Some day you might find yourself cornered in a conversation with me at some literary event, with no ready excuse to walk away, your glass still half full. It's okay. You don't have to look at me when I talk to you. Just listen to the sound of my voice.

DEREK SCHULZ

That's Not a Māori Name: Penelope Fitzgerald's Aotearoan adventure

For Liz Eastmond

I fell for the writing of Penelope Fitzgerald after getting hold of a copy of *The Bookshop* (1978), her short, pithy second novel that catalogued the grinding down of a feisty woman battling to keep a progressive bookshop, along with her idealism, afloat in a conservative English town.

Three qualities worked together to captivate me, the first being the effortless way she infused a radical political will into her work without recourse to polemic. Then there was the wily timbre of a voice that took her out beyond the fictional conventions of the comic novel. Well, of course she could swing a plot around at will, and craft objectionable characters into it to be spit-roasted on cue, but there was always a sense that if you were enjoying this too much, you were missing the point. The intelligence in her tone picked away at your gullibility. Here the UK counter to the *nouveau roman* began leaking through the spurious charms of a Midsomer town as she steered herself with guile and purpose, out into territory where language itself began to falter around her.

So how did she manage that? Here's one way that unfolds early in the piece:

> *In 1953 the cellar had carried seven foot of seawater until the last of the floods had subsided. On the other hand some of the seawater was still there.*

This is disarmingly quixotic and smart because it doesn't simply qualify what looks like a factual statement, it also undermines it, utilising the sway of fiction to deepen the play of meaning around it. The open-ended subterfuge fictionalises the facts. There is more going on here than we are given the detailing to know. And this is where we are being ushered into a world where a final understanding will always lie out of reach. It's not that we don't know precisely what's going on, but that we can't.

You can't write like this by thinking about it. But does this read too much philosophical nuance into her work? No, because here's another:

Gentleness is not kindness.

This differentiates between a human quality that can carry moral ambiguity—gentleness; and one that can't—kindness. And having prodded her reader to keep up, she then illustrates exactly how this difference operates in the character of one of her joyless intriguers. And should you require further evidence, here it is …

The frame of mind, however, is everything.

But where does this come from?

Growing up within her intellectual and theological whānau would have helped a lot, but there's a second source that links her back to Somerville College, the generation of women she stands among and the spirit of their times. These include Philippa Foot, Elizabeth Anscombe, Mary Midgley, Mary Warnock and Iris Murdoch. They are a disparate lot who lived mostly under the shadow of their male peers but worked away at querying their attempts to establish then *man* esoteric outposts, in order to re-ground themselves back in the world.

Perched behind them are two seminal figures. One is the Austrian Ludwig Wittgenstein, who as early as May 1915 had sketched into his notebook the comment *Die Worte sind wie die Haut auf einem tiefen Wasser—A word spins a veil across very deep water* (my translation), from which no one should have been surprised at the subsequent movement in his thinking.

The other weighty mentor is Virginia Woolf.

Woolf has the same disconcerting ability as Fitzgerald to give pause at the end of a sentence while you struggle to pin a precise understanding to it. My interest in Woolf is also personal. I suffered a similar mental affliction to her and recognised it immediately in her characters. She is quite open in her journal about her ambition to trace out the nature of mental illness, and does this first through Septimus in *Mrs Dalloway*. Here she covers her tracks because any direct identification would have brought forth the withering disdain of the cultural mandarins of her day. (I'm speaking from experience.) So she morphs it into a bloke and invests him with shell shock. What follows is a harrowing portrait of a mind hurtling into manic crisis and this was haunting to me, because in writing it she would have risked calling it back—and probably did.

In *To the Lighthouse* the game is moved on apace through the diverting character of the artist Lily Briscoe. She is way more savvy than she cares to let on, and possesses an enigmatic kink in her world view:

> *Could loving, as people called it, make her and Mrs Ramsay one? For it was not knowledge but unity she desired …*

Here desire lurches toward disease because it works to disable love not foster it and, as this spreads into the world around her, it dooms her project to failure. A remorseless pessimism begins to rise. It is with Rhoda in *The Waves*, however, that Woolf has her final say regarding the radical suspicion that the world transcends the boundaries placed around it by a Western imagination; then the possibility of escape from that.

> *I am above the earth now … All is soft and bending … Out of me now my mind can pour …*

Rhoda is tuned by a sensitivity too subtle, delicate and strange to survive in this world, as is made clear early on when as a child, Woolf has her kept in after school to work on her numbers. It becomes apparent that she understands the controlling ambitions behind the idea of numbering only too well.

> *… the loop of the figure is beginning to fill with time. It holds the world in it. The world is entire and I am outside of it, crying 'Oh save me from being blown forever outside the loop of time!'*

She is gazing at a figure 8 chalked on the blackboard, though what she sees is the symbol for infinity: ∞. The whole book circles around a devastating discernment that teases up an intrigue it can neither identify nor fathom. The last thirty pages are unbearable. Mania dangles a very subtle and seductive lure. You have it for life, there is no cure, and while medications and therapy are sometimes useful to stall its progress, the only effective counter I found lay in fighting it to a standstill, then working on strategies to keep it at arm's length. The end of *The Waves*, however, reveals that Woolf has succumbed to its lure. I was successful in keeping it at bay (so far), but it then shifted focus, seeding experiences that took me well beyond normal sensory boundaries and a respectable Western intellectual life.

Fitzgerald also takes up arms against the jurisdiction of numbers, having a child in *The Bookshop* raise the issue, only to make fun of it as the serenely confident ten-year-old Christine Gipping assesses her chances in the 11-plus exam:

> … *they give you numbers, like 8, 5, 12, 9, 22, 16, and you have to say which number comes next … Florence was unable to tell which number came next. She had been born too long ago.*

More centrally, Fitzgerald shares Woolf's determination to remake language in order to move it toward her experience of the world and not the other way around, which is the usual state of affairs. But over the character, necessity and durability of love, the two authors part company. *Mrs Dalloway* portrays a failed relationship that leads to distressing regrets, while Woolf's wistful evocation of a bisexual identity implies that Clarissa's natural sensual self has fallen victim to the mores of her time. Fitzgerald explores sensual relationships with an obsessive delicacy that harbours no illusions, and this takes her into the same fluid territory, which she views from a very different angle—through the experience of suffering. She lacks Woolf's cryptic sensory insight but harbours metaphysical ambitions all the same, which are concealed with a wily English artistry that Hermione Lee opens up in a late interview with the author:

> '*I would want my religion to get into my novels and I'm very ashamed that it doesn't,*'

she confesses. Lee, rifling through the novels, frames Fitzgerald's spiritual inclinations in attractive non-denominational terms as 'a faith without beliefs', which links her back to the 'Honest to God' debates of the 1960s, then Bonhoeffer, Bultmann and Tillich among others. I was born sceptical, however, and while my personal experience had convinced me that we had a long way to go in forming a credible Weltanschauung, I presumed the cautious methodologies of philosophy and of science would prove to be the prudent way forward. It stationed me firmly on Woolf's side of the fence.

But then along comes Fitzgerald with Florence Green and her unconscionable rapper to build a bridge between the two writers:

A faint whispering, scratching and tapping could be heard coming from the upstairs passage … Florence did not pretend to herself, any more than she had ever done, that nothing was wrong.

This was the third strand in the work that caught my attention because here was a serious writer risking early self-immolation by turning her back on titillation and satire in her attempt to illuminate experience with which I was only too familiar. She stood against a feral tide and appeared to be writing from personal experience because suddenly we are pitched out of the fiction and watching a live stream. This Lee confirms:

The terrifying and entirely convincing appearance of a poltergeist in The Bookshop *is also based on life. 'Oh I'm quite sure of it,' she says, matter-of-factly. 'But it's not a high manifestation, it doesn't really lead to anything.'*

Fitzgerald typically elucidates the subject by shutting it down. Then later in her writing life she produced an Aotearoan story, 'At Hiruhārama', which appears to address her spiritual idealism rather more openly than she is prepared to let on. It is set in and near the town of Whanganui, which was our home for twenty-five years, and recounts the birth of twin girls in desperate conditions in a remote farmhouse, as retold by a grandson back in the UK long after the family's return. Though the date is not specified, my guess is around the mid-1890s.

My first response to this story was sniffy, rating it as an early work by an outsider who had never visited the country. Hermione Lee's biography, however, includes a short account of its genesis and this revealed Fitzgerald's creative imagination in mid-performance and showed how her intelligence underscored it. This is not an early story (c. 1992), and *is* written by an outsider who has never visited the country. The blurring in the detail serves her purpose and is true to her narrator. But she also fixes the tone and temper of an English immigrant more deftly perhaps, than local writing can now manage, because this is her tribe, and we've all moved well past the air, qualm and presence of that.

Lee locates its source in an encounter with a Kiwi pilgrim at the Jordan River where Fitzgerald was baptised, and there are too many tie-ins to the biblical nativity story (itself a fabrication) for this not to lie near the centre of the tale, but she marinates her narrative in playful blasphemy. It is Kitty's first pregnancy so she is a virgin in that sense but not the biblical one. The couple manage the birth alone, albeit with a doleful observer. She then goes on to spawn a large family. Fitzgerald is at pains to advise that their dwelling is not a manger, and while Kitty gives birth to twin girls, the more resourceful of the two ends up temporarily in the tip out the back with the offal and the afterbirth, which may or may not be a pithy comment on her professional life to come in a world run by men (she becomes a lawyer). The father is one of Fitzgerald's attractive, intensely focused young males, who floats through the story cryptically aware of the odds stacked against him, while taking steps to pre-empt them, all the while keeping himself civil and humane.

These two parents, forced into work as servants through the happenstance of birth, run with the opportunity the colony provides to lift themselves from servitude, in a familiar colonial narrative. The capable, spirited women in my whānau of that generation had little option but to work as servants, while my wife's grandparents' life in Whanganui followed a similar track to the storied couple. They came out in 1908, ran a general store, produced a daughter (my mother-in-law), and returned to the UK twenty years later because of failing health.

But what has Penelope Fitzgerald done to the geography of our country?

She is careful to point out that Hiruhārama is Jerusalem, the hamlet set on the Whanganui River about an hour's drive from the town of Whanganui. She sets a very false trail, however, in fictionalising the area. Should you follow her directions you would find yourself to the west of the town, on the road to Houhora. Hiruhārama lies roughly north of Whanganui on the eastern bank of the river, which she evaporates, but then alludes to in renaming the town Awanui. Houhora is on the Pacific coast in the far north of the North Island around 700km distant and could not be reached from that side of the river, which makes it too odd a choice *not* to be deliberate. The word might be broken down to hou/hora, feathers spread out, which calls up the pigeons in the story, then perhaps, an angelic presence; but it is also on the road to Cape Rēinga, which tips its cap to a Māori metaphysic, for it is from here that the spirits of the dead set off on their journey back to Hawaiki. Fitzgerald doesn't give much help in pursuing these connections, but in relocating the town of Awanui in Taranaki she is probably unaware that she has outraged the entire district.

The title of this story, 'At Hiruhārama', pitches Fitzgerald into the complex, fraught and culturally challenging territory of bicultural interplay, an area in which I accumulated experience in working professionally with taonga in the Whanganui Museum and elsewhere, and then later in environmental and public health activism. My younger self imagined that such experience would confirm a woven correspondence between the cultures. It proved the opposite. Here two alien world views jostle each other apart, while the Pākehā picturing of its bicultural partner showed itself to be an academic fantasy.

As a Pākehā working in a Māori world you require protective support. It is folly to proceed without it. In 1991 I curated an exhibition for Artspace in Auckland which for the first time brought taonga into our top contemporary art gallery. I travelled to the famous cultural centre at Whakarewarewa in Rotorua to organise the loan. My visit was well received, convivial and successful. I came away congratulating myself on the special qualities I possessed for working in this area; only to learn, much later, that Aromea Tahiwi, the contemporary weaver in the show who had bloodlines connecting her to the local iwi, had been through a fortnight before and done all the work for me.

Four or five of the senior kuia from Tūhourangi came up to the exhibition opening and, to my art-world horror, began picking apart one of her weavings to reset it their way. The look on Aromea's face was one of utter delight. This could throw up great difficulties for the unwary parked back in Pākehā-land. A centrepiece of the exhibition was an intense weaving that the designer wanted moved from the primary wall and replaced by something more eye catching. He was unaware that it carried the mana of the show. It hangs in parliament's committee room and the laborious process of arranging to borrow it for the exhibition had been dramatically short-circuited by Koro Wētere, the senior Māori figure in the Labour Party (then in Opposition). He marched Aromea into the committee room, asked, 'Is this the one?', then hefted it off the wall and handed it to her.

So how does Fitzgerald fare?

'That's not a Māori name.'

The doctor in her story makes this brusque claim regarding the philology of Hiruhārama and he is right; though this is complicated, given the fact that the original composition of written Māori rested entirely in the hands of Europeans. Jerusalem was named by a prominent early Anglican missionary, Richard Taylor, who probably also coined the Māori transliteration. Such words are not bona fide te reo Māori but examples of what I would call pidgin-Māori, a Pākehā language. You hear much of pidgin-English, the sometimes charming remaking of English by various indigenous cultures, but not the opposite, the remaking of indigenous language by settler cultures—an indicator of where power lies in a society.

The name Whanganui *is* Māori. It denotes a wide harbour (an estuary in this case), but in some cases Pākehā settlers who did not speak te reo would tack the suffix -nui onto a word to lend a feature or town local colour. This was an act of placement by immigrants who mostly remained indifferent to, and apart from, the indigenous culture and language. Fitzgerald does this when she remakes Whanganui into Awanui, though from her intelligence, sensitivity and elusive strategising, a rather different aroma arises.

Awa is the Māori word for river, and the directions she supplies for the pigeon's flight back to town from Jerusalem are just about right, give or take a point or two. But the hamlet itself is much further away than she implies, and was originally accessible only by canoe or steamboat. All this geofactual hanky-panky builds a mythology of separation into the story, but in setting it beside the history of Hiruhārama she also calls up the river's intriguing spiritual history.

Jerusalem has hosted two unorthodox Pākehā religious figures of national renown—Suzanne Aubert and James K. Baxter, both Catholics. The more influential Wiremu Rātana experienced the visions that began his ministry, just before the Spanish Influenza epidemic of 1918, down on the coast about 10km south of the river mouth. These were not evangelical missions, but each established in its own way a centre of healing.

Aubert, a French nun, had a nursing background and ran a medical clinic and foundling orphanage at Jerusalem in the 1890s. She developed a range of herbal medicines based on local Māori remedies and was admirably principled. She refused to commercialise her operation and destroyed her recipes when she moved to a new ministry at Island Bay, Wellington.

Poet Baxter opened a community there in the late 1960s, with the support of local Māori. This attracted a wide range of troubled (and not so troubled) refugees from society, including former prison inmates and the mentally ill. It was a short-lived and famously idealistic venture, and Baxter's *Jerusalem Sonnets*, among his most enduring writing, was written there shortly before his death in 1972.

However, the importance of Jerusalem lies primarily with Pākehā. The centres of import for Māori on the awa have shifted over the years but it is the river itself that remains at the centre of their lives. It holds a comparable position to Jordan in a Christian metaphysic—comparable but not equivalent. Māori inhabit a very different world to Pākehā. Te Ao Marama—the world of light—is female and held under the jurisdiction of Papatūānuku. This world is alive and your passage through it needs to be negotiated. The awa is a mentor to the people who live there or trace their history back to it and they don't see themselves as separated from it. This is captured in the whakataukī or proverb 'Ko au te awa, ko te awa ko au'—*I am the river, the river is me.* For local iwi the awa is not outside or beyond human sentient experience. The currents of environmental law, in Aotearoa and internationally, are belatedly beginning to turn in this direction.

It remains a moot point whether Fitzgerald had an understanding of this in renaming Whanganui Awanui. What does seem reasonable to assume, given her scrupulousness, is that the gist of these stories captured her interest. But her narrative strips out the metaphysical costuming and returns to burdensome reality, emphasising the isolation of the couple, the very real dangers involved for mother and babies, and the father's inexperience coupled with his resourceful prudence. She appears to be relying on the history of Jerusalem and its redolent name to imply a spiritual connection, though she never declares it. Where it does surface, its primary quality is a precarious good-heartedness that is perpetually under threat, while remaining nevertheless indubitable.

Virginia Woolf's ambition in *The Waves* was to move language away from the hegemony of semantics and back toward the condition of music; back to the home that te reo Māori never left. Woolf is clear about this where, in 'A Sketch of the Past', she envisages the world as a work of art from which we are indivisible:

> … *we are the words; we are the music; we are the thing itself.*

This is where a healthy female scepticism circling the politics of how we have come to use language to think, begins first to trouble and then to bite. Fitzgerald picked this up, and the gift of a writer working with this degree of subtlety lies not in the recalibration of knowledge, but in revelation. This is anathema to zealots of whatever hue, for she has shown that while the various strands of human understanding might stand in their corners barking at each other, as you rise beyond that, everything turns into a story. And these stories fit together, albeit continuing to elbow each other for room.

REFERENCES
'I would want my religion' … Penelope Fitzgerald talks to Hermione Lee, 'A Very English Genius', *New Writing 7*, 1998, p. 136.
'The terrifying and entirely convincing appearance' … ibid., p. 142.

JUSTINE WHITFIELD

The Klimt Bubbles: Contemplating concealment and connection

I wrote once of the heart in riot, as if the bloom and swell of a pulse should be denied—controlled and suppressed, subdued to a forced state of calm, brought down by electrode and allowed to lie like the blue-tinged tongue of a cattle beast, severed and discarded on a concrete slaughterhouse floor.

There is a bridge on a Louisiana bayou that stretches like the tin-can-coloured shaft of a slide trombone, a thin, flat, pale presence that peels endlessly out across pleated fingers of khaki swamp. Trees wade knee deep in the creased water, touching each other and swaying away, their hair and shoulders a broad festoon of stretching movement, soft hide green against the dull pelt sky. If you do not eat meat out of compassion for sentient beings, you will cross that bridge and wonder about your right to eat plants. The bridge is eighteen miles long. The muted colourscape and the croon of concrete close beneath the car will take you in a cradle song. It will become apparent that time is a long quiet game. All may fade but those trees will remain.

I crossed that bridge this March just gone, on my way to New Orleans. We were a gang of accountants in an Audi SUV, passive participants in profit-driven apocalypse, although nobody else in the car held that view. The driver spoke of Trump. She disliked his personality but believed in his politics. A dirty yellow truck drove past with a pro-life bumper sticker: It's a child not a choice. That afternoon we had stood in a NASA-style control room at head office and watched our company helicopters on giant screens moving above the Gulf of Mexico, small, bright, blinking lights connecting rigs attached like ticks to the ocean floor. The flick of a finger on a keyboard changed the view and we saw the synapse-like network of gas pipes concealed beneath the Gulf waters, soft wild tangles like the twigs of trees but made by man and now rooted unseen to the planet floor.

That morning in my hotel bed I had read an article on The Spinoff urging the New Zealand government of Jacinda Ardern to end oil and gas exploration. It was written by my stepfather. My sense of dislocation was so great it felt ironic.

I work for an international aviation company that services the oil and gas sector. Oil is a villain active in war, carbon emissions and the infusion of plastic into the cells of creatures living in spindle seams concealed beneath the remotest sub-sea cliffs. Oil does not work alone—people assist—but still, my conscience looks like an armadillo: a scuttle of armoured skin with warted welts and self-striped scars. Grate-like gashes open relentlessly but I suture them with thoughts of the men and women helicoptered to work and returned safe to quiet houses where children sit at lit kitchen tables eating bread and reading books bought with their parents' wages.

I sat in that Audi and felt discomfort and alienation. These people were not mine. I was tired and far from home in every sense. Everything of importance was imprisoned within me, held unexpressed in deference to something I couldn't define. I watched the trees and thought of their invisible connectedness; the underground fungal networks that thread individual trees into communities and serve as channels for the sharing of sustenance and warning.

In the French Quarter of New Orleans, outside Pat O'Brien's bar around 10pm, I met a young black bouncer called Caleb. He looked like my brother Nikolai, and I told him this. There was a strange sad moment of tension as he balked at my use of *brother* before realising I was foreign and meant the comment literally. He was skinny and tall with short braids tied in a bun at the nape of his neck. Beneath his smart green gabardine blazer he had that young male scruffiness—white shirt unevenly tucked to concave hips and wisps of hair on his jaw. His neck was covered in an intricate tattoo. I asked what it meant. He said he chose it because he liked how it looked, simple as that. I nodded and made to move away but he held my eyes.

'Here, help me,' he said. Together we removed his blazer sleeve and freed his right arm and shoulder from the thin dress shirt. He showed me a detailed mosaic tattoo—water, sky, hills and wind—that covered his arm and flowed on to his chest.

'This tattoo is about my family and where I come from,' he said. 'And this is the girl I hope to meet one day.' He pointed to a hidden mermaid, teaspoon-sized and elliptically etched to the swell of his forearm, her eyes and breasts obscured orbs surrounded by a helix of hair and tail. I stroked her hair and touched her breasts and told him I hoped he found her. Then I removed my cardigan and showed him the tattoos on my own back. He put his hands down my top, moving the neckline and the back of my bra aside.

'I shouldn't be doing this,' he said.

'It's okay, I'm old,' I replied and we laughed, strangers with our hands on each other's skin.

*

This exchange took perhaps ten minutes but it broke a resolution I had recently made—to refrain from touching strangers and colleagues. I used to touch people freely. Mostly arms or shoulders, maybe a hand, and I have occasionally touched hair. For me, these gestures were as spontaneous and unconscious as eye movements.

In the wake of Weinstein and the beginnings of the #MeToo movement, I read a piece on social media where women in retail and hospitality roles talked about the social touching they experience. While not overtly sexual, this contact was often seen as invasive and entitled, as if the normal rules of respect and separation were not observed and the right to touch the server's body was part of the transaction—the female an obliged receptacle, sashed in place by the employment setting and service ethic.

But resolutions aside, the truth and simplicity of the connection with that young man was also intensely at odds with the alienation and dissonance of my day. I have returned to the contrast over and over again.

*

Poets have no eyes. Poets are taproots, existentially valid only as channels. They stand in silent camouflage, allowing the world to flow across the moth fine filament threads that coat their synapses like fur villi. Through these villi, the ley lines of the universe and all underground streams of consciousness become visible to the poet like veins beneath loved skin.

Through the poet, we own our blood.

*

Touch is the sense that does not erode with age. Touch, however fleeting, bridges physical space and releases chemicals within us relevant to the perceived intent of the contact. Touch is essential for a baby's survival, and skin-to-skin contact improves the prognosis for infants born prematurely. We are touched first by whānau and later by lovers, friends and rivals.

May all things good be present in those spaces. And may the old continue to be held.

*

The most beautiful fact I know is that a Neanderthal was found buried with a flower in her hand. In fact, this may not be a fact. I read it once in a text on human evolution but years later, the text no longer in my possession, I researched it online, hoping to stand again before that beaming shrine of an image. Instead, I read that the early humanoid had perhaps fallen into a depression in the earth and been covered eventually by drifting debris that randomly held flowers.

Depression indeed. In a small act of faith, I reject this cautious interpretation and hold to the original yellow-covered text, issued for a biomedical science paper at Victoria University in 2000. I justify such subjectivity with my belief that Richard Dawkins, and those of his ilk, have made some splendid contributions but are the type of people who would play Scrabble with Freddie Mercury and mind about the score.

That burial tells me that in the earliest cells of our consciousness, before the sophistications of intelligence were overlaid, we felt connection to each other and we understood its loss. Simultaneously we registered beauty in our environment and equated it with the profoundness of connection.

*

Physicists view touch as collision and a condition to physical causality. Theories of causality are interesting because, in philosophy, they undermine the argument for free will and support the non-scientific construct of fate. Science cannibalising science. An exception to physical causality is quantum entanglement theory where particles of matter interact instantaneously with each other, even when severed and separated by large distances.

We do not yet understand how these partnered particles continue to respond to each other without any apparent form of connection. Einstein called this 'spooky action at a distance'. He suspected it indicated a fault in the theory but particle entanglement has since been experimentally verified. The universe is threaded in ways that even Richard Dawkins does not yet understand.

*

August 2017—
National Radio says that there are diamond storms on Uranus. I imagine the remote unknown space, the unseen shining churn, the million globes of crushed-glass blossom that wash like pollen to rest in soft cold seas; flat wide cradles of saltless water made grey and clear by the freckle-red gases that bloom in the tight sky air above.

Perfect Klimt-like storms.

That which we do not see, does still exist. Principles of physics and chemistry apply throughout space. Crush means to minimise under pressure. Carbon in this instance.

Crush is the minimisation of love.

*

I lay in bed with a footballer once and asked what he was thinking about. Arsenal, he said. I said I was imagining how I might paint the world in the negative so that the soul spaces buried behind our known faces were visible and our physical bodies were concealed from view. He guffawed and I made a mental note to leave when the weather warmed. High on the futility, I continued.

If we could see the unseen, I said, we'd notice huge balloons behind each person, crammed with constantly shifting mixes of emotion, thought and memory, infinitely subtle and complex but held mostly hidden. If I was an artist I would paint this as two tiny monochromatic people facing each other at the bottom of the canvas but dwarfed by massive planet-sized bubbles filled with Klimt-like colour and pattern—and each bubble would be jostling against and intertwining with the other person's bubble but also with the billion other bubbles of psychedelic colour present in the world.

'I like it,' he said when I finished. 'But what does *Klimt* mean? It sounds really filthy.'

He was, I said … in the most beautiful of ways … and I left when summer came.

*

Artists often love skin and cavernously seek its connection. I thought this was a bias toward the sensual and a just act of exchange—a pressing and taking of beauty that facilitates the bringing forth of all the artist holds inside. But I watched *Nanette* on Netflix recently and I'm not sure what I think now. In this piece, Hannah Gadsby, an Australian comedian with experience beyond the bounds of traditional binary gender, delivers a stand-up routine that covers art, sex, gender, violence, gender-violence and power. She says that art history shows us, repeatedly, the obsessional painting of females as giant flesh vases for cocks. I enjoyed my shock and later I enjoyed that the complementary adjective for size was assigned to the vase.

But she is right. We rarely celebrate the female gaze. We frequently call it the *mother's gaze* and confine it to the private realm.

*

The men I work with are remote and brutal, in a soft shambolic way that is reminiscent of hippopotami. The blunt force of their short heavy legs can pulp the internal organs of thinner animals but such injuries are not personal. They are casual casualties of the men's hefty swaying amble toward their individual visions of the Limpopo River. Women before me have been crushed. I lean into the boardroom table meetings, like Sheryl Sandberg says women should, trying to be one of the men but also trying to avoid being rolled for breaching unspoken notions of feminine boundaries.

*

The dominant cultural tone of many corporate structures—law firms, financial organisations, oil companies, political parties—is set by the men who have traditionally held power. This tone is necessarily mirrored by the women who have risen to sit alongside them. This culture centres, directly and indirectly, on constructs of profit, growth and competition for resources.

David Yarrow, a financier turned wildlife photographer, in an interview with Kim Hill on Radio New Zealand recently said this of the corporate existence:

> *It didn't bring me happiness. It's fairly one-dimensional because if you're working in a field where you're judged by how much money you make for other people and then the reward for that is money for yourself, the accretion of wealth becomes your soul for the vast majority of your working week which I think leads to certain parts of your character [becoming] sub-optimal for the vast majority of people you yourself hang around with.*

In an evolutionary sense, we may be hard-wired for profit, growth and competition. These actions are linked to the amassing of resources, and my friend Richard Dawkins would tell us that, in evolutionary terms, the amassing of resources improves the odds of success. Individuals with resources were better able to protect offspring to maturity and this signal of strength attracted mates.

The game has changed and the amassing of resources now threatens our survival. If we are to correct our course or avoid repeat on a colony planet, it is now necessary that we bring emotional voice, tempered by intelligence, into the corporate world. We do this by creating cultures where people share what they hold inside—cultures where people do not silently watch things that make them uncomfortable.

*

Mary Shelley wrote on themes akin to this. *Frankenstein* is considered a comment on our tampering with nature and its ultimate ability to destroy us. From a place of soft distance, *Frankenstein* may also be considered a meditation on the misuse of skin written by a young woman unafraid of sexuality. By nineteen, Shelley had held her dead daughter in her arms. She understood connection and her writing underscored the horror that arises where we disengage from touch.

Shelley is known for *Frankenstein* but she wrote other novels. A common theme was the importance of cooperation and connection and she often placed this in a female setting. Shelley spent good parts of her working life supporting the work of her husband, poet Percy Bysshe Shelley, and sometimes other writers. Her work was geared toward enabling voice and the bringing forth of that held within.

Frankenstein is an early example of science-fiction and a woman's vision of horror.

*

We don't eat horses because they are tall,
like supermodels and CEOs.
Cows are short and quiet,
menacing like Gandhi.

I am tall and quiet and people eat me all the time,
but not in the way that supermodels are eaten
—teeth not tongues if you are confused.

*

My present concern is this. As we remove the metaphoric cladding from the people and structures that generate #MeToo experiences, we also risk great loss.

It is right that we remove this cladding. The vast and varied landscape of #MeToo permutations is the inverse of Pandora's box. But as we work to build a safe and equal environment for people of all genders, we also create a vigilance that runs through all exchanges. We spotlight the interactions between genders in corporate and professional settings, and in this glare we will hesitate to touch in any sense.

Connection occurs where we touch people physically or bring forth the truth of what we hold inside. And quantum physics suggests that, once established, connection is transcendent, so powerful that it can be maintained between particles across wide distances and in the absence of any visible link or mechanism for exchange. Remote particles will spin in alignment with their once-entangled twin, and humans will carry forward learning, feeling and memory from compelling encounters. The catch is that entanglement must first be allowed to occur.

Mary Shelley has warned us of the horror that arises when we disconnect from touch.

*

As an accountant working in aviation, my job is to calculate the price that oil companies will pay for our helicopters to land on the rigs that we have attached like ticks to the ocean floor. I use *we* in the collective sense but I am a passive participant in profit-driven apocalypse. I feed my family and buy books with my wages but continue to bide time in spreadsheet cells. I sit at boardroom tables where my quiet voice is over-spoken by men. The confinement and internal conflict feel like a castration of the soul. I am tired and far from home.

Nelson Mandela and Reuben 'Hurricane' Carter have told us that, in true situations of harsh imprisonment, the internal world persists. The soul is less tangible than tissue and it continues to contract long after it is cut. The final freedom is the ability to choose our thoughts.

*

From a bridge across a bayou, I watched the trees and thought of their invisible connectedness; the underground networks that thread individuals into communities and serve as channels for the sharing of sustenance and warning. The muted colourscape took me in a cradle song. Time is a long, quiet game. All may fade but those trees will remain.

JOCELYN PRASAD

Uncut Cloth

Dad brought home some of Mum's clothes when we emptied her room at the rest home. In a spare bedroom downstairs, sagging cardigans hang alongside trackpants and a few musty *salwar kameez*. The sarees are presumably still at the bottom of the dresser. I try to avoid going into the house. Dad, at ninety-four, worries I'll steal their things.

Mum wore sarees to church. Their wonder unfolded on Sunday mornings, when she pulled one of the seemingly endless pieces of cloth from her wardrobe and draped it around her body. She wound, tucked and pleated the seamless garment meticulously. Eye level with her navel, I held the material taut as she folded it back on itself to make pleats tucked into her petticoat. When finished, she would float down the stairs to the idling Hillman Hunter. The car would fill with the sweet scent of clove, her choice of breath freshener.

Mum was the only woman who wore a saree at St Martin's and probably the only parishioner in Mount Roskill whose midriff was visible at Sunday service. The stone-cold church in a frosty Auckland winter wasn't hospitable but Mum had acclimatised. Photographs taken soon after she emigrated from Fiji show her wearing a thick white polo-neck under her saree, with an ochre-coloured cardigan on top. She grew used to New Zealand's brisk climate, eventually reverting to the conventional flesh-baring *choli* (blouse) and insulating herself with a concealed flannelette petticoat, thick and fleecy like my winter bedsheets.

Sarees go back 5000 years to the *dhoti*, a loincloth first worn by followers of Buddha. Evolving to cover women's upper bodies, they were uncut, unstitched and fastened with knots; ancient Hindus believed piercing woven cloth with scissors and needles invited impurity. Between four and eight metres long, the choice of saree length depends on how you want to wear it. And there are dozens, if not hundreds, of different drapes.

Mum chose the most popular drape, the *nivi*. The ritual would start by tucking one end of a six-metre saree into her petticoat, winding it anticlockwise until it came full circle. It's a bit like wrapping yourself in a towel after a shower. Next, the saree's other end was turned into pleats, made along its width. This *pallu* is wound across the right hip, over the left shoulder and fastened to the *choli*. Mum finished off by transforming the saree's undraped middle portion into lengthwise pleats tucked into the petticoat near her abdomen.

A game of sartorial Twister to the uninitiated, dressing in a saree takes two minutes for the most accomplished wearers. It took Mum ten, a little longer on special occasions when the softer printed chiffons worn at church were swapped for thicker, embroidered silks. (Although purists champion handwoven sarees unpierced by needles, embroidered sarees are increasingly popular.)

Sometime between my brother's graduation and mine, Mum stopped wearing sarees. Her fingers, cruelled by arthritis, were no longer up to the required intricacies. And strokes had become an unwelcome fixture in her life. I remember the first one clearly, watching her topple over the heater the night David Lange was voted in. The strokes stealthily whittled away her life's pleasures: lawn bowls, driving, writing, talking, dressing up.

Never overly sentimental, she wordlessly converted to *salwar kameez*, the tunic and pants pairing fashioned by the Moghuls. The complexity of dressing was reduced to a hook-and-eye fastener on the back of the *kameez* (long shirt) and a drawstring on the *salwar* (pants) worn underneath. The hanging sarees were folded and put into the dresser.

Born and raised in Auckland, I was never offered Indian outfits. There was always, instead, a garish best dress bought two sizes too big so it would last. Red and white striped with butterfly sleeves and a sash tied at the back. Pink floral-patterned silk with a white lace collar. It's small wonder I gravitated to black when I started buying my own clothes.

It was during a holiday in Fiji when relatives had me try on a *salwar kameez*. I was fourteen. '*Kaafi sundar larki, nah?*' the women in the store clucked. I didn't see a beautiful girl. I saw a gangly teenager, her big '80s hair cemented with hairspray, in an outfit with too much colour and pants way too baggy. I imagined two of the boys who teased me at school, Andrew and Wayne, and their trademark taunt, 'I am liking it hot,' with faux Indian accents and wobbling heads.

'I don't like it,' I said, leaving the outfit in the fitting room. The women shook their heads but said nothing.

Years later in Wellington, where Chris and I married, Mum tried her luck by buying me Indian wedding jewellery. The pieces were modest by Indian standards, ostentatious by mine (I got around in a pair of stud earrings). The 22-carat gold necklace and earrings, no small expense for a pensioner, were a welcome inspiration for my wedding outfit. Possessing neither a peachy complexion nor a discernible bust I was ill-suited to the melange of meringues on offer at the bridal stores. I opted instead for my own variation of the *ghagra choli*, a long skirt and blouse. The skirt, from an upmarket store, was cut simply and made with embroidered cream silk from India. The blouse was tailored from purple raw silk bought on a work trip to London.

There is no such thing as too much gold at an Indian wedding. Brides have been known to dress in *zardozi* (metal) embroidered wedding sarees, burned after wearing to retrieve their gold. In this spirit, Mum wore an electric blue *salwar kameez* embroidered in gold and paired with her own gold jewellery.

She was as elegant and gracious and delightful as I could have hoped for on my wedding day. But the mother of my childhood was gone. Her outfit sat slightly askew on her stooping shoulders. The long hair she used to gather into a bun had been ravaged by alopecia so she supplemented it with a wig. She shuffled more than she strode, her body battling the cold front that was hitting Wellington. It was a happy day but my heart sinks when I look at Mum in the photos. I'm ashamed to admit it but I'd wanted her to have more sparkle.

Most of the family were living in Auckland when I got pregnant, around the same time Mum had the stroke that delivered her to Gracedale. The rest home was near her house and around the corner from the old St Martin's Church, recently bulldozed to accommodate the southwestern motorway. Furnished in beige and brittle cheer, Gracedale occupied a site that once housed a borstal. Mum and I had been there years earlier when, in a previous incarnation, it had served as a landing point for Vietnamese refugees she helped resettle.

Initially we left most of Mum's clothes at home, at Dad's behest. 'She'll come home soon,' he said, and my siblings and I agreed because we were tired, and it was easier than discussing the intractable truth. One by one the *salwar kameez* moved across to Gracedale for weddings or birthdays or other increasingly rare occasions calling for something other than elasticised pants and zip-up microfleeces.

We moved to Sydney that year, but my baby son and I often flew home to check on Mum. Once, soon after Hari started walking, I took them both to Cornwall Park. By then trackpants and acrylic tops, pilled by Gracedale's industrial washing machines, were Mum's wardrobe staples. Hari's toddling and her ambling were not so different: slow, tentative, stopping at whim to pick up a stick or admire a blossom. The spring sun was warm on our faces and we all smiled.

It was the only time Hari and Mum walked together. Soon after, she broke her leg. She eventually got back on her feet only to be felled by another stroke. It now took two rest-home carers to shower and dress her before propping her into the chair in which she whiled away her days.

Weddings were the glue in Mum's family. They reunited her with siblings and their offspring, now scattered around the world. She was devastated not to be well enough to fly to Sydney for my cousin Navleen's wedding. I stepped up and wore a saree.

I could have chosen a more practical occasion. Navleen and her Irish fiancé James wed on *Sydney Glass Island*—a barge converted into a glass-encased wedding venue. The prospect of negotiating gangways and narrow flights of stairs in a garment that could fall apart with the slightest tug was daunting. But I persisted, in a borrowed deep pink saree embroidered with gold floral-paisley detail and bordered in green.

YouTube was my friend. I watched at least four 'how to wear a saree' clips before the wedding. On the day, my hands shifted between holding the fabric in place and hitting pause on a step-by-step video tutorial. My teeth became a dressing implement. I could have done with an extra pair of hands, like Kali, the powerful black goddess and destroyer of demons.

Now I just needed to figure out how to walk. Each step came with the fear of unravelling. Like a middle-aged fitness freak, I had calculated the day's steps: from house to taxi, taxi to boat, minimal movement on the boat, then back home. Finding a workable gait, I clutched Chris's elbow and shuffled to the taxi, a tentative geisha making her debut.

At Darling Harbour it was impossible to miss the gathered wedding guests dressed in every imaginable colour and flecked with gold like an array of exotic birds. My cousin Anju took one look at me and said, 'We need to fix your saree.' She escorted me, deflated, into *Sydney Glass Island*'s claustrophobic bathroom and silently remade the saree's pleats, tucking them closer to my belly.

Mum would have loved it. Her niece getting married under a bright Sydney sky, the harbour bridge in the backdrop one moment, Fort Denison the next. All against the soundscape of the officiating pandit chanting in Sanskrit. Mum converted from Hinduism to Christianity when she got married but kept a foot in both camps. 'We all worship the same God,' she would say whenever I quizzed her on religion.

'Deep down she was always a Hindu,' one of Mum's sisters told me on the phone the day after she died. We had her dressed in a recently bought pale pink *salwar kameez* for her funeral and invited a pandit to offer prayers alongside the Anglican vicar. I didn't have the energy to think about my own outfit—I wore a black dress that slipped over my head.

I own one saree, bought by Chris as a spontaneous birthday gift from a store called Rups Big Bear in Mum's home town of Lautoka, Fiji. A deep green chiffon, it has, like most sarees, three design elements. The endpiece, used to make the *pallu* draped over the shoulder, is sewn with hundreds of tiny black sequins and stitches to form marigolds in various states of bloom. The border, running along the hem, is a thick band of more sequins. The field, little of which is visible when the saree is worn, is unembellished. Like many contemporary sarees it had a second endpiece, to be cut off and used to sew a matching blouse.

I wore the saree to my cousin Sanjay's wedding last year, also in Lautoka. Prasads had flocked to Fiji from all over the world, taking over the local hotel. Leaving nothing to chance this time, I earmarked matriarchal saree doyenne Aunty Uma to help me. I wasn't alone; when I knocked on her door, there were three cousins queued ahead of me. I'd left my run too late. My sister saved the day, but not before I returned to my hotel room, looked out at the big old palm trees worried by the breeze and quietly sobbed.

'You know you can buy readymade sarees,' Aunty Uma said after the wedding. Recently invented ergonomic sarees come with stitched pleats and *pallu*, an elasticised waist, Velcro fasteners and built-in pockets. They take just a minute to put on.

'But that feels like cheating,' I said. The joy of sarees comes not just with the end result. Like origami or baking a cake, the act of creating is as rewarding as the result. It's satisfying to tuck a saree, making sure the hemline stays straight. To savour the repetition required when making pleats. To wander back on those early memories in my mother's bedroom, with its Formica dressing table, and look through Venetian blinds at the lawn my dad mowed every week with his Masport four-stroke. To recall the off-key variation of *Für Elise* playing on the jewellery box holding the brooches Mum used to fasten her *pallu*.

The time will come when we will sift through my parents' belongings, apportion mementoes, sell furniture on Trade Me. I've earmarked a saree, the one Mum paired with the polo-neck. It's bluish green like clear water on a coral reef. She wore it when she brought me home from hospital after I was born. Who knows what state I will find it in? The moths might beat me to it. I may have little choice but to risk the wrath of the gods and cut it into pieces for cushion covers or a summer dress.

MIKAELA NYMAN

Language Means Belonging

I started singing in a choir in my early teens in an effort to belong. Up until then my only experience of choirs consisted of compulsory music lessons at school. Since then, I cannot recall a time when music and singing have not been in my life in some form. Even those who have never nurtured an inclination to join a choir may appreciate the energy released in the act of singing collectively if they've attended church, watched films like *Sister Act* and *As It Is in Heaven*, or an episode of *Glee*.

My parents had decided to leave the rat-race and Stockholm's suburbia and return to the Åland Islands in Finland, where my father, sister and I were born. It was a move towards a slower and safer life; it offered more family time, a life outside work for my parents, and a reunion with elderly grandparents for my sister and me. Because we had left before I started primary school, however, the islands didn't automatically feel like home for me. Speaking the language helped. Singing helped even more.

Finland prides itself on being a bilingual country. Finnish and Swedish are the two official—if vastly divergent—languages. Finnish is spoken by over 90 per cent of the population, while only 5.3 per cent speak Swedish. (In comparison, 3.7 per cent of the New Zealand population can hold a conversation in Māori about everyday things.) Both languages are compulsory in primary and secondary schools, and citizens have a legal right, at least technically, to be served in their preferred official language when dealing with government authorities and banks. In addition, there are several minority languages, including Finnish Sign Language, three Sami languages, Romani and Karelian.

Blessed with family on both sides of the main language divide, I've never resented having to learn both languages—in fact on the contrary. Language is much more than a communication tool.

*

Once the playground of Swedish kings and Russian tsars, and the site of an unlikely Crimean War in the 1850s, the Åland Islands, situated midway between Sweden and Finland, aspired to peace and independence. In 1921, only four years after Finland declared its independence from the Soviet Union, the Åland Islands gained autonomy, demilitarised status, and even their own parliament and flag. Most importantly, they were granted the right to speak and conduct their affairs in their preferred language, Swedish.

For small island communities, whether located in the Pacific Ocean or the Baltic Sea, the provision of quality education and viable career paths will always pose a challenge. But the Åland Islands' location meant we had access to educational institutions and job opportunities in Finland and Sweden. At a time when there was no choice but national TV on offer, we could watch both Swedish and Finnish programmes. The only cinema in town sported an enormous screen, as the foreign-language movies required two sets of subtitles—guaranteed to cover up any nudity happening at the bottom of the screen.

*

On 6 December 2017 Finland celebrated its centenary as an independent nation-state. While Finland, like New Zealand, is a young nation, its languages are older than man-made boundaries. One of the most revered Swedish-speaking authors, Zacharias Topelius, was writing Finnish history in Swedish two centuries ago when Finland was a grand duchy in the Russian empire.

My teenage self was desperate for a community, for belonging, a streak I recognise remains strong in the adult me. As a fourteen-year-old I established a vocal quartet, consisting of my best friend, my sister, her best friend and myself. I played the piano and sang alto, and made the others stand on their chairs and aim higher when they couldn't reach the top notes. The thrill when all four voices came together, the harmonies taking us beyond our own limitations, more than made up for my still being an outsider at school.

Over the next few years Estonian independence activists would demonstrate the power inherent in song and in their ancestral language by singing down the Soviet invaders in remarkable acts of non-violent resistance. Forbidden to speak Estonian in their daily lives, they sang songs that drew on nineteenth-century poetry, folk tales and founding legends, songs that were as familiar to the

Estonians as nursery rhymes or the faces of their grandparents. It united and inspired people to stand up against their oppressors.

Had my maternal grandfather still been alive on 6 December 2017 he would have rattled his weapons from the Winter War and celebrated Finland's centenary by lighting a candle, playing Sibelius' *Finlandia*, indulging in an unhealthy quantity of alcohol and reminiscing about the wars that did not cease with independence.

*

In *The Summer Book*, acclaimed Finnish novelist and cartoonist Tove Jansson, of Moomintroll fame, wrote, 'A very long time ago, Grandmother had wanted to tell about all the things they did, but no one had bothered to ask. And now she had lost the urge.'

In an increasingly mobile world, it's not only urge and opportunity that are at issue. There are questions of literacy levels, and whether different generations of the same family even speak the same language. All these factors determine whether family stories, ancestral legends and indigenous knowledge are passed on to the next generation or lost along the way. Grandchildren tend to be interested in their grandparents' stories. If nothing else, they're incredulous that the older generation managed to lead a life worth living without computers, mobile phones, iTunes and Netflix.

'You must have been so bored,' my children say to their grandmother in Taranaki when she reminisces about social dances and modest suppers in her youth—simple entertainment *sans* gadgets.

*

Tove Jansson was my hero from a young age; she still is. When I arrived in New Zealand in 2002 with a seven-week-old in my arms, I looked to the musicians and writers for orientation. I discovered Janet Frame and Keri Hulme; then I found Patricia Grace, who opened a door to a different world, with people, communities, stories and language that was specific and mattered. Her stories were an integral part of the place in which I'd chosen to set down roots and bring up my family. Each of these writers scratched at the cultural varnish, exposing what lay hidden beneath, providing insight into a society straining to find its shape.

The Moomintroll books opened up a world that was in equal parts familiar and imaginary, a world of philosophical musings, great humanity and adventures. A world I've in turn relished sharing with my children, in Swedish, in books and animated film form. Many times I was told off for speaking Swedish to my toddlers because I was 'confusing' them. I don't think they were ever confused. At a café in Stockholm my daughter, aged three, ignored her breakfast, so amazed was she on hearing everyone speak in what up until then had been Mum's secret language. After that she began initiating conversations in Swedish. However, with no one her own age to communicate with, it didn't last.

Tove Jansson was born into the minority Swedish-speaking population of Finland, as was I. The island environment she describes in *The Summer Book* with its peculiar smells and sounds is achingly familiar. In her writing she showed that language matters, with all the familiarity it evokes, including its symbolism, idiom and implied meanings. Indeed, the landscape, the seasons and the language shape the humans they cradle. As an adult, peeling off the layers of the onion created by her storytelling genius, I discovered another version of the stories I'd loved as a child, a darker side to Tove Jansson's philosophical musings and metaphors. Her critters may be imaginary, but their characteristics and behaviour are inherently human, something adults and children alike can relate to.

We all need to see ourselves reflected in writing, film and the arts, and language is the starting point.

*

In my thirties I started singing in a choir in New Plymouth in an effort to belong, in an effort to find myself. Arriving in New Zealand with a newborn baby I felt extremely lonely, the separation from family and friends laced with a bout of post-natal blues. I panicked when my well-meaning mother-in-law suggested it was too early for outings, that I could join a choir later, when my daughter was older. Singing became my rebellion, in a small way. The weekly act of singing in the Central School hall saved me. The joy of harmonies knitting together … Unfamiliar songs soon became familiar territory.

A few months after I'd joined I was greeted in town by a fellow choir member who recognised me as Mikaela from the choir, not as Steve's partner, Em's mother, or Valerie's son's Finnish partner. Only as me. A functioning, creative person in my own right.

These days our local school is small and the enrolment is about fifty–fifty Māori and Pākehā. My boys are learning te reo and kapa haka to an extent their New Plymouth-born dad never did. The whole family has enjoyed the annual Puanga in Waitara, where the wāhine presenting the Taranaki talent are fast talking and witty. The boys' school has done extremely well in the primary schools' kapa haka competition. Their world is expanding, and language and singing are a big part of this. They embody a way of thinking, of being, of growing as an individual and as a community, a nation even.

After all this time away from my ancestral islands, I worry about losing the dexterity and vocabulary of my mother tongue, perhaps even a part of the wiring of my brain that makes me who I am. I'm grateful for online magazines, books, brilliant 'Scandi noir' TV series, and the existence of Viber and Skype. I think I've regained some vocabulary I lost over the years thanks to these technological advances. Just don't ask me to translate my own poems.

*

Lagom is the quintessential Swedish word meaning just right, just enough, everything in moderation. It applies to individuals, behaviour, desires and things. You could say it's the ethos of the whole Swedish nation (said tongue in cheek; Sweden and Finland have a similar big brother–little brother relationship to Australia and New Zealand). A margarine called Lätt & Lagom, meaning Light & In Moderation, gained popularity in the 1970s despite the fact that it thinned to resemble body lotion when left in room temperature. As so often is the case, there's more to the word *lagom* than its literal translation implies.

Due to the quirks of language, I find translating my own writing a near impossible task, whether it's fiction or poetry. The creatures inhabiting my dreams speak in different languages. The language I've chosen to write in rules my thinking, the expressions and images I lean towards, the tone and style, the humour embedded in the narrative, the underlying references to ancestors and historical events, the sensuality of the words themselves and how they're strung together. In this regard English, Swedish and Finnish each have their advantages and shortcomings.

Penning a simple poem to my sister, who died five years ago, playing with English, Swedish and Finnish words, I find it resists translation: the tone and rhythm conspire, irony falls flat, turning it into weak tea. A different poem altogether.

Lagom finns inte	*Lagom* **doesn't exist**
Att bekänna sin kärlek på engelska är inte hälften så allvarligt som att älska på sitt modersmål.	To confess your love in English is not half as serious as to love in your mother tongue.
Vad är väl ett slitet poplåtslove mot att älska eller rakastaa?	What's a worn pop song love compared to *att älska* or *rakastaa*?
När man älskar någon så hårt finns det alltid risk att något går sönder	When you love someone so hard there's always a risk that something breaks
ett hjärta, till exempel, vilket i och för sig är jämförbart med ett broken heart.	*ett hjärta*, for example, which actually is comparable to a broken heart.
Det är så svårt att älska lagom.	It's so hard to love in moderation.

I have the highest regard for skilled translators. Short of being able to enjoy the classics in the original language, we all have to rely on translations, or various applications that mangle language by taking it apart and reassembling its components into something that may be far from the intended whole.

When the Korean novelist Han Kang won the 2016 Man Booker International Prize for her novel *The Vegetarian* (*Chaesikjuuija* in Korean), the first of her novels to appear in English, the translator, Deborah Smith, gained widespread attention for her 'flawed yet remarkable translation'. A few allegations surfaced of mistranslation, omission and misidentification of the subject of sentences, while some who had read the original in Korean claimed that Smith had rewritten the whole novel. That her style—formal English, with lyrical flourishes—took over, providing a different experience to Han Kang's spare, fragmented style. Smith's defence was that she stayed true to the spirit of the text as she perceived it.

Should a translator stay true to the literal words or to the spirit of a text? These two different approaches are at times irreconcilable. Whenever I've read several translations of the same work, some brilliant, others mediocre, it sparks a longing to know the original, to glimpse what the author intended. Even though the author's intention remains open for interpretation, like everything else in literature. Nouns are not merely nouns. A sponge cake doesn't sound as generous as a sugar cake, or as extravagant as a lace cake. It depends on the social context and the memories conjured up by that cake—whether it was a sweltering day, whether a baby was born, or a brother stung by a wasp submerged in the sticky icing. To anyone attempting a shortcut, I'd say, don't you dare translate my sugar or lace into a sponge.

*

The formulation of language starts before we even know what the words mean. It starts as whale song in the mother's belly, followed by nursery rhymes and lullabies. I'm indebted to award-winning Swedish writer and translator Lennart Hellsing and his nonsensical nursery rhymes for a lifelong enchantment with playful language, sound and rhythm, something I later encountered in Dr Seuss. My first French words at age six emerged as song, possibly 'Frère Jacques' or 'Sur le Pont d'Avignon', while my first English consisted of merrily rowing a boat ashore as a nine-year-old. I still remember the songs.

Recently I found a documentary from 2011 on Māori oriori, or lullabies, with respected kaumatua Amster Reedy. The programme originally screened on *Waka Huia* on New Zealand television and can be found on YouTube. Talking about his extensive research into traditional Māori oriori, Reedy emphasises the importance of lullabies and the need for babies to hear their own language, or languages, in the formative years, and how oriori can be used as a framework for raising children and strengthening whānau. He raises salient points about the developmental and wider social benefits of singing.

Being part of a waiata group at work, learning songs together with the accompanying movements that reveal we are part of a wider Pacific family, has felt like learning a different language twice over. It's in stark contrast to the Nordic approach, where only mouths and eyebrows move, with the occasional sway. In my few years in Vanuatu, it never ceased to amaze me how songs and performances connect people across linguistic and cultural boundaries, nationally as well as regionally.

Cultural and linguistic freedom are inextricably linked to power relations in society. Among our Pacific neighbours, Vanuatu, with a population of about 255,000 and over 130 vernacular languages, has undertaken significant education reform. After seventy-four years of colonial administration, and thirty-four years as an independent nation state, the use of vernacular languages in the classroom is finally allowed. Until recently the official languages of education have been limited to English and French. Work has been under way since 2010 to prepare for this major policy shift. In September 2017 a literacy specialist at the Curriculum Development Unit in Port Vila told me that reading resources for Years 1 to 3 had been translated into fifty-nine vernacular languages, as well as Bislama. Vanuatu has embarked on a brave path to ensure the focus is on children's development and learning, not on the learning of a foreign language.

Nevertheless, laying down a nation's bilingual intentions in law and in policy is just the start of a long journey. The past year or so has seen an unprecedented surge in Pākehā in New Zealand wishing to learn te reo, resulting in a shortage of teachers and long waiting lists for courses and night classes. The Wellington City Council is discussing more Māori sculptures, and street signs and café menus in te reo. The Green Party and the Māori Party are advocating for compulsory te reo in schools, with the Māori Party also keen for Māori ways of knowing to be included in the curriculum.

The government's current policy only calls for 'universal availability' and integration of te reo into the primary school curriculum by 2025. The prime minister has specifically avoided the word 'compulsory'. What may seem like semantics is nevertheless an important distinction.

Meanwhile, a sign-language interpreter has appeared by the prime minister's side, adding a new dimension to her press conferences, and gifting her with a 'sign name' in a gesture that makes New Zealand Sign Language more visible. In due course perhaps we will learn through a gesture when 'universal availability' becomes 'compulsory'.

JANE BLAIKIE

Mrs Wakefield, Unknown

What to make of the New Zealand coloniser Edward Gibbon Wakefield in the surge of fourth-wave feminism and #MeToo?

Wakefield set up the New Zealand Company, which was the colonising vehicle in and around Wellington and Nelson, and is a daily namesake: Wakefield Street, Wakefield Park, Wakefield Hospital. His bronze bust on top of Matairangi-Mt Victoria. His reputation has been hammered by decolonisation but not enough to question his memorialisation.

Does his little-known abduction of the child-heiress Ellen Turner and their illicit marriage merit more debate? Criticism of his activities as a coloniser can be tempered by the notion of 'presentism'—he was 'of his time' in the project of empire—but even by the standards of his day the Ellen Turner affair was shocking.

Wakefield had a shifting story to account for the abduction, which occurred when he was thirty. From a large Quaker family with intellectual interests but failing fortunes, he had an obstinate and silver-tongued personality that led him to flout convention from a young age. He refused to return to one school and was asked to leave another, and by age twenty had already eloped with an heiress, ward of court Eliza Pattle, coming into a decent fortune by this means.

This marriage was reportedly a love match—Wakefield described Eliza as 'perfect': she was willing to become his 'own creature, whose mind would in time take just what impressions I pleased'. But Eliza died after four pregnancies and the birth of their second surviving child, Edward Jerningham.

Wakefield spent his married years and several following, along with wads of his marriage settlement, in trying to overturn Eliza's father's will and gain more from it, while also working for the British legation in France and Italy as a kind of apprentice diplomat. He was a determined networker and, obsessed with entering parliament, he needed a lot more capital. A seat had to be bought, by way of a patron, and then the requisite lifestyle of an MP funded by a large private income.

His legal battle over the will eventually failed, and during the Christmas of 1825, passed in the overheated salons of Paris with his brother William and his ambitious young stepmother Fanny, various new plans and schemes were floated. Wakefield picked up on an improbable suggestion of Fanny's and persuaded his companions to its feasibility. They would trick a neighbour of Fanny's back in England, whom Wakefield had never met, into marrying him.

Ellen Turner was the only surviving child of William Turner, who had property from cotton mills, and she was also sole heir to her uncle's fortune from silk and banking, all totalling about half a million pounds—in today's money, something like $NZ80 million. William Turner had brought his family south from Lancaster to Cheshire and had just built an impressive neo-classical mansion. The move was likely made with the intention of distancing Ellen from the districts in which she was known as having come from 'trade', and securing a match for her among the gentry. She attended an academy in Liverpool where young ladies learnt the skills necessary to run large households and raise genteel families.

In early March 1826, three weeks after Ellen's fifteenth birthday, Wakefield borrowed money from his stepmother and bought a flashy carriage, a green barouche. On the morning of 7 March he sent it to Ellen's academy with his French servant and a note purportedly from the Turners' doctor. The note said Miss Turner's mother had become paralysed and she wished to see her daughter immediately. Ellen did not recognise the carriage or the servant but the sisters who ran the academy were persuaded to their legitimacy by the servant, who claimed to be newly employed by the Turners, having previously worked at a neighbouring estate. He had been well briefed on details of the Turner family.

Ellen set off in the barouche, which stopped to pick up the Wakefield brothers. Edward Gibbon explained that the note had been a ruse—the actual crisis was that her father was the victim of a bank failure. Over the next twenty-six hours he hurried Ellen north, with William riding outside in the box. The story evolved as they galloped from inn to inn. Wakefield's wealthy uncle was prepared to bail out William Turner, but only if his nephew became Ellen's husband. Otherwise her family would be ruined and turned out of the new mansion. They swayed and bumped through the night and were married at Gretna Green.

From there, they travelled south. The barouche broke down at Carlisle and they had to switch to a public conveyance; in London they stopped overnight, then crossed to Calais. The whole journey had taken five days, with two nights travelling and three nights in hotels.

They lingered in Calais. They must have been weary and Ellen may have refused to go on until she heard from her family. More particularly, however, Wakefield awaited the arrival of an old friend, Algernon Percy, who was due to land on his way to Switzerland as British ambassador. Wakefield planned to travel under his diplomatic protection. But Percy arrived a day too late.

In defence of his actions, Wakefield would initially tell Ellen's uncle that she had been 'represented to me as a fine girl, with the largest fortune in the country, and I was therefore determined to possess myself of her … I have never attempted anything I did not accomplish.'

When it became apparent the Turners would not fall in with his scheme, Wakefield began to claim he was disinterestedly defending her father from vicious local gossips who, he had heard from his stepmother, were deriding Turner as a vulgar parvenu. A gentleman like Wakefield would bring honour to the family.

Wakefield's Quaker grandmother seems to have understood her grandson best: 'His obstinacy if he inclines to evil terrifies me—turned to good it would be a noble firmness.' Perhaps, then, there was an autistic bent to his character, an obsessive rigidity of thinking and a failure to read the broader social situation?

William Turner first heard of the marriage when he read the announcement in *The Times*. In the initial shock and disbelief—as far as he knew, his daughter was safely at school—he thought it might be a cruel hoax. But he feared the shock would kill his wife, who was not well. When the horrible truth became clear, he threw all his resources into recovering Ellen.

Wakefield, meantime, sent an unctuous letter to Turner introducing himself as Ellen's new husband. He wanted it both ways: the heiress and approbation. He had discovered he rather liked Ellen, and he wanted her family's good regard as he shaped her into his ideal wife.

Turner remained in England, too distressed to travel, while a party of five—Ellen's uncles, a Bow Street officer and two lawyers—set out for Calais. They carried a warrant for Wakefield's arrest and a despatch from the Foreign Secretary to the British ambassador in Paris seeking his assistance.

When Wakefield was sprung in Calais, he made no attempt to detain Ellen. He wrote to his brother William, who was still in England, saying he had made a 'merit of necessity' and 'let her go'. Ellen's uncles had insisted on seeing her privately, and once she was told the truth she fell into their arms. She is reported to have said, 'Oh! He is a brute! He has deceived me! And I never called anyone a brute before!'

Wakefield stayed in France to arrange his affairs, then returned to England where he began an energetic campaign to have his bride returned. He published a 7000-word letter disparaging the Turners for forcing their daughter into a protracted legal process—William Turner was 'striving to make his daughter a public laughing stock, and the object of everlasting curiosity and comment'.

Wakefield believed his hand was strong because Ellen had agreed to spend nights with him. Never mind that they were as 'brother and sister', as he had formally declared to the Turners; the very fact of such unchaperoned company was enough to generate a scandal, which he assumed the family would wish to hush up. But the charges against him went ahead, despite speculation in the press that the Turners would buy Wakefield off in return for an annulment. When Wakefield eventually handed himself in, he was indicted with a felony for which he could have been executed. It was later downgraded to a misdemeanour.

He claimed he had no anxiety about going to trial, because of Ellen's agreement to their adventures. In Calais he had bought her new clothes and 'was so fully occupied in teaching, dressing, amusing and caressing the high spirited and affectionate girl … that I was indifferent to almost everything but the actual enjoyment of the moment [of] which no one can imagine the intoxicating nature'.

A contemporary portrait shows Wakefield's light wiry curls swept into long sideburns framing regular features, intensely focused eyes and a determined near-smile. Newspapers called him a 'belhomme', though his elegant clothes suggest a touch of dandyism. His secretary, Charles Allom, would later write that he was 'a master of the art of persuading, he seldom failed if he could get his victim into conversation'. Perhaps Wakefield's bad luck was that the only room in which he was able to get within talking distance of Ellen's father was a courtroom.

Ellen herself appears to have remained relatively composed during the abduction. Bank failures were not uncommon. A schoolfriend at the academy she had attended (but did not return to) had had to quit it a few weeks before the abduction when her family's business and reputation had collapsed. Ellen understood the imperative of action in such a situation, and there may have been some truth to Wakefield's claims she enjoyed the escape from school.

Wakefield fought each step of the court proceedings. While on bail, it was said he could be seen walking in the Turners' neighbourhood, and he sent Ellen a Christmas gift of love poems. But the Turners were having none of it. They spent £10,000 on lawyers.

After fifteen months of contested court proceedings—ruinously expensive for the Wakefields—a jury found brothers Edward Gibbon and William and their stepmother guilty of conspiracy, and the brothers were each sentenced to three years' prison.

Then the marriage could be annulled by an act of parliament. During the annulment proceedings Wakefield, cornered and about to lose everything, let slide his smooth manners. He suggested the marriage was real: 'My wife married me through love and affection.' He claimed she had spoken of her father's violent anger, and that when they were alone in the carriage they had done nothing but laugh and kiss. He implied Ellen had lied in court. He hinted that the marriage may have been consummated after all.

But Ellen, who appeared at all the hearings, remained steadfast. *The Times* described her as 'rather above the middle size, a good figure, with large dark eyes and what is generally called a pleasing face, her appearance modest'. She delivered her evidence almost without hesitation. She had only consented to the marriage because she believed it necessary to save her father. And she was believed by her family, the courts, parliament and a public gripped by every detail. Hotels near the courts were booked out for weeks, and the courtrooms were so packed, the high-society ladies who would not be kept away sat up next to the judge, that being the only space available. *The Times* put out a special edition to report the verdict. Ellen was reported to 'have the manners of a highly finished lady'; 'there is something so fascinating about her'; and 'her fine form and figure are peculiarly commanding and her manner altogether bespeaks a more than ordinary share of intelligence'. Wakefield, on the other hand, was 'base and mercenary'.

Yet during his years at Newgate Prison, Wakefield made inroads in recovering his reputation. He rented a reasonably comfortable room: 'my cook, slut and butler … is an Irishwoman' (such a servant could be hired for as little as a shilling a week). He read widely and wrote compassionately about the horrific conditions suffered by the poor in jail, which included rape, murder, disease and hunger. He highlighted the case of one young man, condemned to death, who climbed a pipe and injured his legs jumping from the prison wall in an escape attempt. The youth had his injuries attentively treated by a surgeon before he was carried to the gallows with his legs in bloody bandages. Wakefield came to believe the death penalty did not deter crime. His observations were published as *Punishment of Death in the Metropolis* and favourably reviewed in *The Athenaeum*. He wrote too against slavery.

From there he turned his thoughts to overseas territories as a way of alleviating pauperism, and published *The Art of Colonisation*. He looked first to Canada, then New Zealand. Once again he involved family. After leaving jail, Wakefield's brother William had become a soldier of fortune (mercenary) in Spain, but in the late 1830s he took up Edward Gibbon's invitation to work for the New Zealand Company, of which Edward Gibbon became director in March 1839. Edward Gibbon remained in England but William arrived in Wellington in August of that year and embarked upon dubious land deals with Māori to buy large tracts on both sides of Cook Strait (and would spend much of the 1840s fighting in the courts to prove their legitimacy). Another brother, Arthur, would be killed at the Wairau incident. Edward Gibbon's son, Edward Jerningham Wakefield, arrived at age nineteen to begin a long, slow decline into alcoholism and poverty. (Jerningham's sister Nina had died from consumption a few years earlier. While Edward Gibbon was in prison, he had insisted his children live nearby with a governess and visit him daily, despite the pleas of his sister to send them abroad. It's hard to imagine how Nina, of whose sensitive temperament Wakefield wrote eloquently, endured the Newgate visits.)

From England Edward Gibbon managed the political side of his projects ('wire-pulling' at the Colonial Office), although he made several trips to Canada and was briefly elected to a Lower Assembly there. He suffered a major stroke in 1846, from which he slowly recovered, and in 1852 decided to visit New Zealand, ostensibly in search of rest and to see the results of his efforts in practice. Historian Miles Fairburn has speculated that it was more likely he wanted 'to take up the illustrious political career barred to him in England'.

Soon after arriving, he was elected to the Hutt seat for the House of Representatives and threw himself into a new series of schemes, winning enemies in parliament while playing a populist hand to his voters. He was brought low by a chill, caught while driving home to Wellington from a constituent meeting in the Hutt, and developed rheumatic fever, which forced him to resign from the House. He fell into a deep depression and for the last seven years of his life stayed home with his German manservant and two favourite bulldogs, seeing virtually no one.

In 1990 Fairburn generously summed him up by saying the qualities that allowed him to deviate from the norms of acceptable conduct also enabled him to be an intellectual innovator. Wakefield has not been so kindly treated by the scholarship of decolonisation but his disfavour has not been so great as to prompt the renaming or reworking of geographical namesakes.

Ellen, meanwhile, has all but disappeared from the record. Does it matter? After all, she was one of any number of English heiresses that Wakefield might have chanced on. But then again, another heiress and her family might not have pursued Wakefield so vigorously through the courts. He may simply have picked the wrong heiress. If he'd picked the right one, would a bust of Wakefield lurk today in a dusty corner of the Palace of Westminster or would his upstart, anti-social tendencies have got short shrift in his own culture? Do children play football at Wakefield Park in Wellington because Ellen Turner was feisty enough to hold her nerve—and should that be better known?

After the court proceedings, the Turner family seems to have just shaken its feathers and moved on. Within eight months of the annulment Ellen had married a neighbour, Thomas Legh. Legh was a bit sullied himself, reputation-wise—he was one of seven illegitimate children of the previous Lord of Lyme Park (all to different mothers) but had been legitimised by an act of parliament and was worth £600,000. The marriage of the Turner–Legh 'capital estates' may have been in the pipeline before the abduction. On her wedding day Ellen wore an Esterhazy silk dress with a white hat and veil and 'looked remarkably well'. Church bells at local villages rang all through the day and the groom's many tenants had a substantial dinner. Ellen's uncle treated his workers to a half-day holiday, with two fat beasts and twelve sheep slaughtered for the spread.

But the marriage ended in a funeral monument, showing the family as classical figures in relief on white marble—Ellen is guided to heaven by an angel while her weeping husband looks on, holding his infant child. Ellen carried three pregnancies to term in thirty-three months, giving birth to two stillborn sons and a surviving daughter. She died a month short of her twentieth birthday.

Thomas and Ellen Legh's family home, Lyme Hall, built in the Italian palazzo style with a central portico, is well known in popular culture in New Zealand and elsewhere as Jane Austen's Pemberly estate in the BBC's cult classic *Pride and Prejudice*. In one scene Fitzwilliam Darcy (played by Colin Firth) returns there unexpectedly on a hot day, takes a plunge in a nearby pond, and then stumbles on Miss Bennet, who happens to be sightseeing with her aunt.

Miss Bennet's visible shock at Darcy/Firth clad in wet linen provides a sexually charged moment that reflects the third-wave feminism of the 1990s when the series was made. Jennifer Ehle, as Elizabeth Bennet, when asked how long she has loved Darcy, clearly relishes the lines: 'It's been coming on so gradually I hardly know but I believe I must date it from seeing his beautiful grounds at Pemberly.' It's all quite deliciously girls-can-do-anything, throwing off the blue-stocking, uptight baggage of first- and second-wave feminism.

Twenty years on, feminism as #MeToo is more about opposition to sexual harassment and rape culture (in particular, via social media). Sexual mores are realigning, assuming the culture-wars backlash wanes. But, surely, to look to the past requires some respect for how things were. Does it matter that by today's standards, the price the privileged guilty paid for their crimes can seem very small?

What is clear in the Wakefield picture is the strange reality that the popular culture images of Ellen's home as Pemberly are so much better known in New Zealand than the remarkable story of her abduction by Wakefield, without which New Zealand's European settler history may be quite different. Besides Wellington and Nelson, the New Zealand Company also acted in Whanganui, Dunedin, Christchurch and New Plymouth.

Looking back to Wakefield, is he exonerated because he did not rape Ellen? If he had done so he may have been hanged. But even by committing the abduction, he was guilty also of a more virulent form of misogyny than prevailed in Austen's England. Is there a compounding effect: the crime; his impervious disrespect for women in general; the pathological, unmanaged, genetic traits of his personality; the retrospective views of decolonisation and feminism?

But out of this, too, comes opportunity.

If we accept Wakefield as a historical face on which Pākehā can project their European past, then he is also a means to help untangle some of the current cultural tensions.

To return to Colin Firth, the actor of the third wave: not so long ago he was temporarily separated from his actual wife, an Italian film producer, and she was reported to have had an affair with a journalist. She has since returned to Firth. Publicly, Firth seems fine with it (not so the journalist). Firth's artistic appeal, as in life, appears anchored in the nuance of a man who does not always have to be first.

Can't there be stories in New Zealand with more nuance? Isn't that part of maturity? To echo the poet Allen Curnow, Pākehā are well past 'landfall in unknown seas'; something is known of 'the trick of standing upright here'; but some gaps are obvious: it's about how Pākehā place themselves.

So yes, the naming of places and public monuments does matter.

A bronze mask of Edward Gibbon Wakefield is fixed to a wall on the 1939 centennial memorial on Matairangi-Mt Victoria overlooking Wellington Harbour, ironically, set there not long before Curnow wrote his landfall poem that signalled a shift away from colonial thinking. Should Ellen Turner have her own memorial in Wellington, a kind of tomb of the unknown female—Mrs Wakefield, unknown? Should an entirely new kind of monument replace the centennial memorial? These questions seem urgent.

Instead of using the high ground, literally in the case of Matairangi, to hold on to an obsolete narrative of arrival, adopting a richer story that embraces Wakefield's flaws would be the means to more open dialogue: one that acknowledges the relatively late arrival of Pākehā, who of course were flawed; one that levels with tangata whenua; one that renews the story and keeps then and now alive. The memorial seems well due for a makeover—its fascia crumbling, the paintwork stained and an apostrophe missing in the text panel: 'The City took the name of Wellington from the Great Duke who assisted the passage of Wakefields Australian Colony Legislation through the English Parliament.' Ouch.

ACKNOWLEDGEMENTS

Miles Fairburn, 'Edward Gibbon Wakefield', from the Dictionary of New Zealand Biography: www.TeAra.govt.nz/en/biographies

Philip Temple, *A Sort of Conscience: The Wakefields* (Auckland: Auckland University Press, 2002)

Kate M. Atkinson, *Abduction: The story of Ellen Turner* (Blenkins Press, 2002)

Abby Ashby and Audrey Jones, *The Shrigley Abduction: A tale of anguish, deceit and violation of the domestic hearth* (Sutton Publishing, 2003)

'William Wakefield', New Zealand History Online: https://nzhistory.govt.nz/people/william-wakefield

KIRSTEEN URE

Pūriri Moth

Here is the green ghost moth, the year my friend died—or the year before. Big as a bird, wings the colour of the apple that could be at the bottom of my school bag. Hammering at the window near my parents' dining table, whole-bodied and urgent.

Now, here I am a few seconds before, my fingers fluorescent with effort, my feet on the linoleum. This is the dining room as it used to be: floor pockmarked with small circles. Beneath my fingers, books and lines of pinkening text—*Othello* quotes, Bahasa vocab. Things to be committed to memory then released the moment an exam supervisor says 'Pens down, please'.

A bright bulb hangs above me at the table—the only light on in the house.

The dark wall to my left is really a window. Through its glass: an invisible suburb. Glamorgan Drive and all the others erased by midnight. This is before the renovation, before the tea trees grew thick and close and a neighbour's child told my parents their home was a tree house. This is a time when, in daylight, this window gives us bush, the rectangles where other people live, snake streets, the sea and, further still, Rangitoto's upturned arms.

From this window too is the pūriri tree my mother planted. An unassuming tree: big enough, leaves dark and glossy, bark soft and flaked. It hosts the ghost moth's grubs. These tunnel into the trunk and live there, buried, for as long as five years (an eternity, it seems to me).

The few lights on outside, down the hill, across the streets, are blurred. My glasses have already gone to bed. Thin and golden, they sleep at the bottom of my bedroom drawer. Without them, each light out there has a circular haze that I don't bother to notice. I squint. Likely, my left eye crosses inwards, focused on the shape of my future: the University Bursary exam, and the books in front of me.

If I have the year right, my friend is not just ill. The school has held fundraisers. His parents have exercised their last chances. They have spent every cent on hopes: a clinic in Mexico, a Reiki practitioner. These are just the ones I know of. I will understand better twenty years after, when my own child dies. If the plastic school ruler at my elbow could give a measure, this night would be past the twenty-ninth centimetre for my friend. But I am not yet eighteen. So I cannot imagine this is an end.

*

I have only been to one funeral. It was held at the beginning of this same year, for my Great Aunt Doreen. If you asked this me, the one studying at the dining table, I would be able to recall two things from that. I could tell you about the man who spoke, uninvited, listing neighbours who'd lived on Doreen's street when she first arrived in New Zealand, but said nothing about Doreen. I could also tell you (but I would not) about the boast I made to my cousin—that my grey Mazda Familia was well accessorised. 'My car rocks,' I said. Nine months after Doreen's death those words already make me wince. I have said goodbye to my dream of becoming Alicia Silverstone, though I have not removed the faux cowhide covers from the Mazda's seats.

Here, I cannot imagine the future is this next funeral. At Schnapper Rock, at the service for my friend, I will shed tears on the shoulder of the teacher neither of us liked. I will sing alto notes in the choir leader's curious performance selection: 'Amazing Grace' and 'Java Jive' (*I love coffee, I love tea, I love the java jive and it loves me*). The day before this, I will decline the request of my friend's parents that I speak, because I don't know what to say or how to be truthful.

Ten years later my grandmother's funeral will be held in this same room, with the same outlook onto the small man-made waterfall. Then I will speak, because then I will have learned to splice truth together into something warm.

*

At the dark window now, the crack of a white-furred abdomen—the pūriri moth, ghost moth, pepe-tuna. The noise as it slams the glass is shocking. It might make my jaw snap in surprise. I might taste the salt-iron blood of my tongue. Perhaps my arms jolt and send the highlighters clattering to the heel-marked linoleum.

Inside the moth's wings, on its underside, the parts I can see seem to have their own luminescence. It appears soft, mossy. Watching it feels like watching a dream. It doesn't look like something that belongs in the place I live. Later, I read it has no mouth, no way to ingest food past its caterpillar stage. It will live like this for only a few days.

It cracks against the glass for a few more beats. Then it flies to the kitchen window, to find another way through. It slams against the glass there, trying to reach me. Though really it just wants the light. From my seat in the future, I wonder whether I might have opened the door, to give the green ghost the thing it craved.

Of course not. Without the glass between us it would become something different: terrifying, insectile. Its insistence, its flap, its size would have me shrieking up the hallway to wake my parents. The following year I will drop casebooks on the large furry spiders that make their home in the frame of my bedroom window. Tonight you could still unsettle me by mentioning the praying mantises—not one but two, the same green as this moth, legs barbed, heads swaying, eyes golden like cats'—that stepped out from beneath the arm of the couch to my school-skirted knees (and their fate) two or three summers ago.

There is only one reasonable thing to do and I suppose I do it. I walk to the doorframe, press my finger to the light switch and tiptoe up the darkened hallway to my room, to my bed.

*

Half a lifetime later I will take my five-year-old daughter to the zoo. This me, the woman who packs lunch and water and raincoats, will be a version of the girl at the table. Some days I will wake, in her body, proud of the tracheostomy scar in the hollow of my neck. A thin raised charm, for luck, for life—but only mine, not my child's. Other days I will hide it under my fingers when I speak. Then I may think of my friend and his parents.

The morning will be a wet, Auckland one. My daughter and I will take refuge in a white domed tent. Inside it will be an exhibition on insects. Here we will fold paper into butterflies, flying them up and away in a plastic tunnel. My daughter will be intrigued by a video of a jewel wasp injecting venom into a cockroach's brain. Her eyes will grow wide when the cockroach becomes a living, edible host for the wasp's eggs. The display that allows her to be the wasp, to push a stinger into the head of a model cockroach—grotesque, the size of a human baby—will capture her attention until the worst of the rain is over.

Just before we leave I will see the ghost. I will pull my daughter towards its pinned body in a circular display. Next to it, other colossal Lepidoptera—the soft, winking wings of a brown Hercules moth, a black butterfly that seems to be made of ink and velvet—will dwarf the pūriri moth. Smaller, less green, the real insect will pale in comparison to my twenty-year-old memory.

'Look,' I will say anyway. 'A moth like that used to come to the window at Dee Dee's at night.' My daughter will be wearing the cardboard mantis crown given to her at the entrance. It will have slipped over her ear and the antenna on the same side will be bent and waving. She will nod and the bent antenna will nod too. Perhaps I will touch the scar on my neck. But I will not be able to show her that I am thinking of her sister, or what I really mean.

Glenfield

I saw Petra in a theatre.

The bellows of the place were empty. The crowd had filtered out to join the hum downstairs and I hung around with my friend Jenna, flicking through Instagram.

She didn't call my name down the aisle. She appeared in front of me, backlit, sidling past my knees. She erupted 'Hi!' like I'd been waiting for her.

I took too long to reply, searching until I landed on her husband's heavy brow bone. I recognised him from her Facebook posts. Petra arranged herself from the blank features.

'It's okay! I look so different.'

She didn't look that different. She was blonde now, and she held herself like she belonged. I smiled big and leaned in.

'How are you? How are your babies?'

I rolled the word over in my mouth and it was obvious. But Petra was gracious. They soon went back to their seats. I didn't mean to do that.

I really, really hadn't recognised her.

*

The last time I'd seen Petra was at Westlake. We had both got in from out of zone. She had brown hair pulled back in a ponytail, held off her face by a stretchy headband. She stood a different way.

She wasn't wearing school uniform. It was mufti day. When we were fourteen, everyone bought their clothes from a shop called Supré. It was a huge place in the middle of Takapuna, lined with racks of tube dresses in every single colour. They gave you your purchases in a hot-pink cloth bag, and you kept it forever. It was the perfect vessel for a netball uniform or a change of clothes after hockey.

Petra was wearing a ra-ra skirt and a mint-green t-shirt. She had little green plastic studs in her ears. I knew exactly how that skirt felt because I had one just like it. The elastic yoke hugged your hip bones and the two tiers were flimsy. They always flipped up in the wind, showing the crease of your thigh. You had to hold it down at the back a certain way. When I think about Petra, the backs of my legs feel cold.

After I saw her I had a strange feeling. It was the same as when you leave your umbrella at the bus stop. You have a hand free where you didn't before, and you can't immediately think why. Your guts flip over and over.

A Supré bag had gone missing, see. From Madison Osborn's hook in the swimming-pool changing room. It was her mufti for after hockey. A ra-ra skirt and a mint-green t-shirt. She had told everybody by lunchtime.

*

I was waiting in a bus stop once. In Glenfield, where I used to live. It was two stops away from our house, but it was next to the dairy and had better graffiti. I used to look for tags by the boys I liked.

It had been raining hard, and the concrete was clogged with bright white litter. Envelopes. A mailbag had split and all our post had blown into the street. On the bench in the bus stop I found the waterlogged pages of a letter. The words were exposed. Insides on the outside. The bus came before I could decide what to do.

*

The place I live now is far from Glenfield. Well, it is and it isn't. At night my bus snakes along a silent ridge. On one side, deep in a valley, is the bus stop next to the dairy. You can't see it in the dark but you can see street lights hovering in the air. On the other side are our warm, new houses where fires burn.

When I saw Petra, I saw Glenfield spelled out in the air. I realised I hadn't heard anyone say it in a really long time. I rolled my eyes around the G, around the loops in the f and the d. For the rest of the play I let my tongue switch over each syllable, turning the memory on and off.

*

They used to send us home with a box of Dairy Milk. We had to sell it and give the money to school. The boxes were heavy and completely untouched.

We knocked on doors in the evening. I held the chocolate in its cardboard briefcase. Boys roared past in cars and I gritted my teeth. Dad waited on the road with the dog while I walked through the dark to each doorway.

In every house I interrupted a little scene. Most people bought one or two bars. I tripped into a dog kennel and fled. His bark tore strips off me.

The last house had tall plants on the doorstep. No shoe rack or dog bed. My dad said he installed the stove in this house. It belonged to a man who was a flight attendant.

Some front doors are very hard to get to—concealed by screens or overgrown hedges. The man kept me there until I started to shiver. Talking and talking about how I didn't have shoes on.

*

There's a specific danger which is ours. You could go missing walking home off the bus. You could find your convex eyes reflected in a little glass pipe. Fuzzy images of yourself on the back wall of the dairy.

You disappear like smoke or you incline towards menace.

You kick away.

*

When Madison told everybody that Petra had stolen her clothes, she told me especially—because Maddy had lived next door to me for as long as I could remember. Our mums talked on the phone all day, mirrored in each others' kitchen windows. We listened, and that's how we learned. They often had the same clothes on the washing line.

*

Our mums took us to swimming once a week. We went to the leisure centre behind the mall in Eileen's Sigma. If we couldn't all fit, someone would coil into the footwell.

We practised swimming to the surface. Pulling ourselves up with our arms while we kicked down, hard.

In the changing room, Korean women got dressed in the open. My mum did not. Eileen asked her if she had a golden box.

*

If you swim hard, you can slip through. If you watch carefully, you learn tricks to help pull yourself up. I slipped through easily because I was good at reading. I got a job in a bookshop where the customers had slipped through before they were even born. Petra slipped through too.

*

When Petra walked away, I told Jenna the story about the mufti day.

I am still kicking so hard.

JESSICA MACLEAN

Strange Harbours

The river of time, as we tend to experience it, flows in only one direction, and often carries flotsam and jetsam downstream, where it can obstruct unwary travellers. How far back upstream must we travel to find the origin of this detritus? (And what future lies waiting, i ngā wā o muri, in those days behind us and thus yet unseen?) Perhaps we trace the striations of whakapapa back to Māui, he who slowed the sun and sought to destroy the Great Maiden of the Night in his last and greatest act of insolence.

And let's not forget Adam, who ate from the cursed tree, thereby gaining the sly insight to blame Woman for the transgression that expelled them (and us) from the Garden of Eden; were it not for their actions, we might all be deathless still. How futile to seek immortality when none had yet died! And what use is perfect knowledge to innocence? Was Hine-Nui-Te-Pō wrong to crush Māui, her most intransigent child, between her obsidian labia? And how pointless to disobey God's single instruction to leave that damned tree alone! Was He wrong to bar the way with fiery cherubim, that we might never return?

Other denizens of the deep exist; why else are so many taniwha aquatic? No other medium is more apt for comparison and metaphor. Sometimes benign, sometimes these taniwha are dark and malevolent. It is not that these entities are necessarily bent on our salvation or destruction; such assumptions over-privilege our position in the natural order of things. Rather, and worse, they are largely indifferent to us, as the mountain is to the ant; their nature and motives remain obscure. This is not to say that they cannot be propitiated, only that we are incapable of perceiving them, as faeries and godlings everywhere fade from prominence in this retrograde age of materialism.

It is more likely that the contemporary influences we apprehend stem directly from Io, the source, and more prosaically from ancestral ghosts and the dark arts of that House of Lore known as Tai-Whetuki. What is natural is good, in the sense that when all is proceeding in a satisfactory fashion, little effort need be directed towards achieving particular ends. Go with the flow; move with prevailing forces. When the tide is against thee, other measures can be taken. Conciliation of ancestral ghosts is reasonably commonplace (and how they haunt us now!), and devotees, often unwitting, of Whiro and his dread minions are legion.

But as to the aforementioned taniwha, and the so-called departmental gods, Tāne and his ilk, representing, *apparently*, the personification of various natural phenomena, they are now somewhat removed from the immediate pressures of day-to-day life, largely because we have absented ourselves from the natural domain, preferring our edifices to artifice over our subordination to the organic. How we chafe at bondage to forces beyond us! We have mastered our fear of Nature through Her defeat at our hands. Mere biological imperatives, faugh! [Insert syllables of disgust.]

The Cartesian divorce of mind from body relegates femininity to the dark and warm recesses of the flesh, never mind the nether regions of the soul. He may think, but does he *feel*? Does he *know*, deep in the gut? The inexorable glare of reason fixes us with its dispassionate gaze; ask any desert creature how pitiless the sun can be. But I digress. Somewhat.

Tāne is the personification of light and life; he sought the uha and imbued Hine-Ahu-One with the breath of life, thereby twinning the ira tangata, the human essence, with the ira atua, the divine essence: inalienable hybridity. Tāne is thus the Father of us all; to this day we retain that divine spark. How far it has fallen, though! How dim that glimmer, an echo that is more a memory than a sound. What remains to recall it now?

Uncles such as Tāwhirimātea and Tangaroa can be utterly remote or terrifyingly present, while Tū of the Contorted Face is surely the most like us, despite our embryophytic paternity. Like his protegés, he eats of the flesh of his brothers. Little more can (or should) be said.

But as for our mothers, aunties and grandmothers, in the mitochondrial channels etched deep in the genes, in the throbs and pulses generated through the aeons of deep time, up past the amygdala through the anterior cingulate to the pre-frontal cortex and then on into the pineal, from Hine-Ahu-One the Clay Formed Maiden, to Hine Titama of the Dawn, to her self-directed and consciously embraced apotheosis as the great Hine-Nui-Te-Pō, oh our mothers are with us still!

Hine-Nui-Te-Pō, formerly the innocent Dawn Maiden, gave birth to her father's children. (Incest prohibitions abound in mythology—just ask Oedipus.) Was she destroyed or disempowered by this? Not even remotely. She, who forbade Tāne from pursuing her, instructing him to remain in this lesser, compromised reality, transcended to a higher, or at least greater, dimension: Rarohenga. Ever a sanctuary for women, as Niwareka will attest, Rarohenga lies beyond Te Rerenga Wairua via a short descent down Te Aka's centuries-old roots (a path I will take one day, when I leave my bones behind at the urupā).

Let us also consider the celestial precinct of the māreikura—Te Rauroha. From here Tāne derives one of his many epithets—Tāne-Te-Wānanga. In his guise as the progenitor of knowledge he ascends to retrieve the three kete mātauranga, all of which he duly entrusted to humanity (and in which basket lay the apple?). But then again, Murirangawhenua had both an upper and a lower jawbone, *only one of which she gave to Māui*. Who was the wiser?

I suspect the worst thing about expulsion from the Garden was the terrifying removal of protective tapu, leaving one exposed to the vagaries and sundry whims of the spirit realm; oh heavenly Father, why hast Thou forsaken us? We wander in the desert, without succour.

All is not lost: although we may be ignorant of them, our mothers' mantle covers us still; oh and how they *grieve* for us; oh and how they hold us in their warm embrace. What are instincts, anyway, but the embodied wisdom of old wives' tales? (How else do we apprehend primeval terrors never directly experienced?)

What epigenetic (and other) teleologies are brought forth from the historical baggage we've accumulated along the tributaries of our shared inheritances? Oh Mother, shine a light on me! Let me be free to differentiate, to potentiate, to articulate ... oh but these words are absurd [laughs to self], and how quixotic an endeavour is this, to write, to speak? Oh that Camus would laugh all right, whistling right past the graveyard, yes and Sartre and Kierkegaard and Nietzsche and all the rest, those dead white men, those exemplars of the higher fucking planes of culture—well fuck you, and you, and you too, but *not* the horse you rode in on, because I, the beast, I the flesh, oh I *feel* you, you fellow sentience, you horse you, you are not your ostensible master, no; imbued with sapience, you have no need for speech. Innocent and ignorant, you rejected that divine fruit, knowing already the rot at the core of that particular apple, instead remaining in the Garden, while we humans occupy the lands east, to varying degrees, of Paradise. How to repent for the sins of forebears? How to scrub out the stains of inherited malaise? (For the fathers ate sour grapes, and the sons' teeth were set on edge.)

How to reclaim the ineffable nuances of a culture that refused to calcify the numinous by way of an adherence to written forms? (The universe is ever-moving, and if we do not move with it, we are forsaken, a dancer with two left feet.)

Much tapu knowledge was simply lost to the world, borne away on a silent and darkening tide, to perhaps wash up on some brighter shore very far from here. Some things indeed pass from the world forever, never to be seen again, as anyone who has lost a loved one can tell you. And even if such knowledge was revealed, how likely is it that these men, these anthropologists (justificatory complicity of the academe), steeped in the cultural and religious brew of Victorian England, were capable of recognising what it was? We Maaris (more often 'bloody Maaris'), we with our *privilege* [sneers contemptuously], our handouts, our over-representation in the justice and health systems, our diminished life expectancy, our treacherous impertinence in our refusal to acquiesce, to let you smooth our dying pillow and go gently into that Good Night and other clichés, you prince of Christ's College, you king of Fen*dal*ton, you who came, saw and conquered, because what's tax evasion in comparison to benefit fraud anyway? [#IamMetiria!]

What's receiving stolen goods (namely, the intergenerational proceeds of the theft of *an entire fucking country*) compared to those other, darker inheritances of shame, grief and terror that manifest in all the usual ways? Aue, aue, thrice aue! Why can our institutions (begin to) admit what our individuals cannot, that the pervasive misdeeds that blight our past are deeply rooted in the personal as well as the systemic?

And what of Christianity? Much is made of the swiftness with which Māori adopted (or appeared to) the religion of a radicalised brown-skinned man, while the identification with the plight of the Israelites is largely (and conveniently) elided; nobody wants to be the Pharaoh (although candidates for

Moses abound). And yet someone must be responsible for … well, everything. Isn't that what gods are for?

Times change. Social media is our new religion; ennui *and* hubris distilled to a mere 140 characters lol omg wtf #InvertedPanopticon. The cult of the self is relentlessly publicly performed, and the means of surveillance and display are made by slaves, paid for by the consumer and heartily endorsed by corporations and governments everywhere—the TV watches us watching it and don't forget to swipe your loyalty card.

Like I can talk anyway, not quite the famously apathetic Generation X but tragically too old to be a Generation Y or Z, missing the generational wave just like my sucker parents, too young to be Boomers, coasting in the wake of the greatest generation and generally favourable global economic conditions, with free education and life-long careers in manufacturing and the public service and low house prices with hypergains to be made (eat the young!), even if you needed a 20 per cent deposit and interest rates were high back then but too old, my beloved parents, brimming with compassion and wisdom and grief, too old to be tech geniuses or slick entrepreneurs in this modern gig economy because who needs a regular payslip, superannuation and sick leave anyway when I can Uber my rides, Airbnb the spare room and bootstrap my way to billions from start-ups and pay the rent with exposure dollars from unpaid internships and achieve simultaneous orgasm every single time because robot Jesus will save us, hallelujah, provided we maintain the settler dogma of hard. fucking. work. and *personal* responsibility and deferred salvation and hastily consumed alcoholic beverages and clumsy sexual assaults masquerading as intimacy and the game starts soon and mustn't forget the bracing influence of fresh air, physical exercise and discipline? Lest we forget Gallipoli [salutes];

[throat-slitting gesture] *Lest we remember Parihaka!*

[insert pūkana of epic proportions]

Now, have I sprinkled enough references, enough sly nods and winks, enough oblique and self-congratulatory allusions to better and more famous works; have I thoroughly demonstrated an understanding of the sociological factors in articulating a site-specific, historically constituted account of Self as continually Produced, Performed and Contested; and have I saliently touched upon the complex and interrelated factors of life in a converging and accelerating digital reality such that I may indulge in my own reflections on where the river of time will take us next? *Have I proven my worth?* This queer half-breed, this singular waveform propagating throughout space-time like a shout, prone to magical thinking and pathological delusion; this human, this survivor, this daughter of Hine-Nui-Te-Pō, I?

Is it strange to think of myself as a miniature New Zealand? Oh but I am. Contained within me are the multitudes, all present and accounted for: denial, the clash of cultures, the good intentions, the destructive tendencies—yes, all there. Schizophrenic straddling of two worlds; sometimes I cannot compose my face or modulate my tone, and find myself hunched in strange rigid postures. Once I come to myself I can move of my own volition, but where am I when I'm not here? Where do we go when we go away from ourselves?

We are stuck. If we cannot go forward, or back, we must go UP; guess our only hope is to construct new waka.

Just as the great double-hulled Te Māmaru traversed the vast reaches of Moana-Nui-a-Kiwa, navigating skilfully using the stars, currents, winds and tides, these new waka will traverse the vast reaches of Moana-Nui-a-Rangi. Golden sails will unfurl for miles, riding the proton winds and gravitational currents, as electromagnetic spray beats upon metallic hulls and the centuries wash by. Instead of the Pacific islands, we will stop at Matawhero, red-faced Mars, then Titan, Parearau's most hospitable satellite, before venturing out into the interstellar depths. What new taniwha await to guide us in to those strange harbours? A plaintive cry rises through the rigging: Mangonui, will we find you there?

Papatūānuku Herself will become the new Hawaiki, the precise location of which can now only be surmised; Hawaiki has escaped the earthly plane and attained the status of myth because of it, which means it can never be destroyed. Distant descendants will trace their whakapapa back to Earth: 'No Papatūānuku āhau!' New suns will need new names, and become a new layer of whakapapa: 'Ko Tama-Nui-Te-Rā te rā!' New maunga, new awa, new stories await us there. Out there, perhaps, we will at last be only humans together; out there we can be one.

Hoea hoea rā! Let us sail ever onward!

TRACEY SLAUGHTER

Notes on a Scale of Silence

I've been to a place where writing doesn't matter. That's a hard fact for a writer to admit, a source of shame. I want to tell you that I've never doubted words, never once let go of their lifeline, never flinched from an unshakeable belief that language is all we have to feed us, bind us, keep us vulnerable, lend us any kind of grace. But that's not the truth. The truth is: I've been to a place where I lost my faith in language, where I knew words didn't count. I lay and looked at a world where if I wrote or not, if I spoke or not, it didn't matter. And the truth is that I stayed there for a long time.

I know the exact moment I reached that place. I can still feel the sound of it. They are wheeling a woman out of surgery into the bed-space next to me, a blue-green vinyl oblong that has been waiting, gleaming and sterile, for her to come around – after the doctors have scalpelled down through her breast tissue, lifted it away, studded the cauterised hole with cleats, a stagger of neon stitches. I can see her face. She's a middle-aged but still hip woman, a tinge of faded punk to her, still a bit rogue in her chopped rose-burgundy hair, a metal half-moon of piercings she had to pick out pre-op, let them clink on the bedside unit like dud ammunition. There's still a bit of mean in her acrylic eyes, a touch of tough bitch, smile armoured with blood-black lipstick.

But that was before, when she'd first arrived, with an equally dark-tinted friend, strode in her nine-hole cherry-docs to my bed and said, 'So what are you in for?' Self-conscious prison-style, smirking. Now they have razored around her breast. They have traced along its trail of glands. They have severed fibres and feathers and cells. They have had to take more than anticipated—they will draw the curtain around her to tell her this later, a futile scrape of privacy, the soft-pitched neutral grind of steel rings dragging the drape on its one-track hopeless halo. They will not be sure they got it all. I will hear the whole thing. She's beside me now, post-op, still sunk in the remains of sleep, laced with tubing, the spikes of her hair sweated quiet. She's a thin frame, flattened and shunted and wired. Ticks and beeps pipe liquid into her, and drain it. She breathes, in the undertow, child-sized, in her electric ligature.

I remember looking at her and knowing this: nothing I could say, or write, could make a difference. Nothing could reach this place we both lay, couldn't touch it, couldn't change it. Words were nothing here. They didn't count. Language was a pointless thing I'd once believed in. Before I came here. Before I confronted this.

In the foreground, as I look over at her, there are books and a notebook stowed on my locker. My husband has brought them in for me—because I am a writer, words are who I am, what I do, so surely they will be the way out. I just need to keep touch with the words. But I don't. I don't even pick them up. The books lie still, thick and new, and I don't open them. The truth is that it hurts me too much to hold them—I've come to the stage where, physically, I can't turn the pages, I can't hold a pen. There's no position on the bed where my body isn't burning, where my vertebrae don't feel racked, code-red. But worse, I think that what's inside those books no longer matters. Those marks on the page can't reach into this place, so why would I ever add to them?

I don't know if this is the night I hear 'What a Wonderful World' played over at the pub, a good-old mongrel local on the corner facing the hospital and the church—a karaoke session at the Salutation that spills piss and wrong octaves and bitter violins, *the colours of the rainbow so pretty in the sky*, onto the pavement. I know it's not the first night I'm wheeled in, when a troupe of spry Christian ladies set up a keyboard in the corner and clap through a medley of trembling hymns, and leave a bright Jesus-loves-me basket propped on my locker, pat my forehead with a flannel they've crochet-trimmed. I know it's not the evening the palliative care team come to brief the old girl adjacent to me, to explain to her with appropriate pamphlets that she'll soon be shifted to a place to die comfortably, even though she has no clue she is terminal; the doctors haven't been yet to pass on the results of her surgery. It's not the evening she steers her beautiful creased gaze over the ward at me and says, 'I've always had a box inside me, where I shut up things I don't want to look at, and turn the bloody key,' kicks off her mangy slippers and flicks out her light, stoic, final.

I know it's not one of the nights this constant supply of gutsy old ladies chirp at me about my handsome husband, my fine young sons, try to chivvy me to keep my chin up, I'll get home to them; I know it's not the first time I answer them with nothing but tears, because I can barely push my body past its pain enough now to respond to my loud treasured sons when they're visiting. I know it's not the first night I am loaded with morphine, but it's one of the next, or the next, or the next, while I lie and wait for my vein to thread its quick uphill suck, for its sideways flex across my heart chambers, so I feel their borders defined in its broadside flood. For the respiratory drop, which is like my gravestone being lowered down onto my ribcage, its slab dark and prone on my near-extinguished breath.

On the first night that terrifies me, and I think I will die under the weight, but I learn to let go and sink with the drug, learn to listen to the shallow chafe of my own oxygen as if from a distance. I learn to collapse, give in to a lot of things. I have gone beyond using my words to point out I'm afraid, I'm in pain, an unthinkable level of pain, the kind of pain a body cannot be in and not feel as an emergency. There is no way to say this. The pain has now stretched on for months and can't be found or fixed. I woke up one night of my settled, steady life and collapsed, and seized, with an unknown virus; unkillable pain up the nerves of my spine is its legacy. Nothing can be done to stop it. I have gone beyond believing there is help. And I learn that for some here in the small-town hospital where I've landed I've even gone beyond sympathy.

So I learn to let the ward nurse scour my chart, disgusted, at the end of the bed, her mission each morning to put a stop to what she sees as malingering. She'll sometimes even make a point of hissing interjections at the doctors on their rounds, underlining that the findings are all negative, the tests keep coming back blank in blood and light, and without a diagnosis the efficient thing is to ship me out—this bed is needed for the recognisably sick. And look at me, don't I still look whole?

I learn to keep my number to myself when asked to locate my pain on a one-to-ten scale—'a *nine*', today's nurse scoffs. 'I've done a hard day's work on worse than a *nine*.' I learn to say nothing. I learn to swallow the pills tipped into the little frilled cup, although they're different from the ones prescribed yesterday, and the next rostered doctor will disagree and switch me back—telling me this colour could trigger Parkinsons, that shade disintegrate my bones. I learn not to say the pills do nothing anyway. I give up saying they do not kill the pain; in fact my body seems to turn the pain dial with each new dosage, forcing the nerve signals up, red hot and shrill, over the block. The first time I stammer this out to a doctor he pats my hand patronisingly, saying, '*My*, you have a lively imagination.'

I learn not to use metaphors to try to describe the pain because the next doctor will only roll his eyes at me and tut, 'I haven't the slightest idea what you *mean*.' I learn to sink. I learn to sink in the therapy pool, when the physio, convinced that action is called for, that vigour, movement and aggression are the principles that will save, grasps my sagging straps and flips my featherweight onto my back. But the muscles of my spine, which are now so much scorched string, cannot even find the power to float.

I learn to spasm, I learn to rattle—and I learn not to quarrel with departmental logic when we beg them to let us rent a hospital bed to take home, because the slanted surface is the only way I can avoid the tremors now that my sinews are wasted. We'll pay, we'll pay money we don't have to get me out of here, we'll pay anything, but we're told a firm no. My age is against me—I'm not over eighty—and quite frankly I don't qualify; put simply, I'm not dying.

I learn not to complain when the curtain is not drawn before a riled nurse strips me down, shoves in an enema, so the man across the room who is browsing a magazine while ignoring his mother can watch. I can lie and cry, and he can watch. And I learn that the pills do the same to everyone else on the ward—turn our insides to stone—so I can hunch in my cubicle and listen to the old man in the next stall weeping as he strains, rest my head on the partition between us and listen to his pitiful shitless keening, and say nothing. There is no point to saying a word. And my husband is learning too. He is learning there is no point bringing me back here after I'm sent home, and sent home, and sent home, yet we have to come back because the pain is still building, still streaming up my spine. I can no longer hold my head up. The feel of the shower on my skin is like nails, the rubbing of the seams of my clothes sends me signals that the joints beneath are being dragged apart. The nerves call SOS, the muscles thrash and lock. But there's no point coming back here.

The next doctor will only shake his head and say, 'I don't understand what it is you expect me to do.' And my husband will go beyond words too, will sit in the ER and answer the doctor by crying.

The worst thing, the thing I am not telling you, the thing I am most ashamed of is: when they wheel in the woman with her breast removed, kohl sponged off her eyes, denuded, coils plugged into the side where her life's been sliced, there is a moment when I envy her. Because she has a diagnosis. Because she has a wound to show. Because her pain has a visible cause. Because there is some kind of treatment. Because around here people respond with some kindness when you are tagged with a legitimate label. Because her condition might be fatal—and I know by now that if I have to go on living in this level of pain, I will not want to.

To my unending guilt, there is a moment when I want that last word.

*

We all run the risk of finding ourselves suddenly delivered to this place beyond words. As simply as I awoke one night, and walked down my hallway feeling strange, and suddenly slipped off the tracks of my life into a long bleak stay in pain, anyone can follow. That blue-green vinyl bed-space beside mine is waiting for anyone to be wheeled in. You 'emigrate to the kingdom of the ill', as Susan Sontag reminds us, at bewildering speed, with a sudden jumpcut in your daily reality that twists it to unrecognisable blur, and any human citizen, at any human moment, is open to this terrible eviction from their bodily home. You can't defend yourself. There is no wall. You are welcomed, in a split second, into this desert. 'Everyone who is born holds dual citizenship, in the kingdom of the well and in the kingdom of the sick. Although we all prefer to use only the good passport, sooner or later each of us is obliged, at least for a spell, to identify ourselves as citizens of that other place,' Sontag writes. And when you wake up in that other place, you're introduced to a hidden population, to the nameless, and stricken, and voiceless rows of people who have vanished from the functioning surface, from the visible operations of society, from what W.H. Auden called 'the common world of the uninjured', what Virginia Woolf termed 'the army of the upright'.

The citizens of that other place have been there all the time, alone, remote, in pain. And the truth is that often they have no tongue. They have no agency.

They have no advocate. They have reached that point that I reached, even as a writer—fast, dark, soundless, final—where they have given up all hope of words. What is the use of words in the face of this? What can words do? What do they even matter? Physical pain, as Elaine Scarry reminds us, is the ultimate destroyer of language. The reflexes of speech are struck silent by it; it leaves us trapped and mute in an experience that at its very essence is resistant to utterance, cut off, inaccessible to words, inherently unshareable—because while for the person in pain the experience is the ultimate in certainty, for the witness to pain its unseeable, unprovable status can represent the ultimate in doubt. Words fail at this gap, and with them, all too often, empathy. 'Let a sufferer try to explain a pain … to a doctor and language at once runs dry,' said Virginia Woolf. Even those whose powers of language seem to pour poetry straight from the bloodstream can find themselves paralysed 'when the lights of health go down', as Woolf knew only too well, can find themselves uprooted, silent, lost in the 'undiscovered countr[y]' of the ill, rendered dumb by its unsayable waste and blight.

*

But for this very reason it matters that those of us who go there try to force that wordless place into the light—that we try to recount our descent into its nightmare state, that we stare hard at the desert of days or years when we were stranded there, that we try to track any frail first step that started our lonely journey back. It matters that we fight the narrative that allows us to speak about affliction only when we can do so from a safely restored place of triumph, courage, resistance, overcoming, return—because some of us do not come back, or never wholly; some of us have to stay, overstay, or live at least some of our ongoing days slipping in and out of its shadows. We may have no stories of heroism, valour, deliverance, cure or conquest to tell, no easy mottos of rising above to slap on an inspiring new-age bestseller. We may only have our knowledge of the dark to share, the confession that we went under, it defeated us. It matters that we are not shamed. When years later I read John Updike's line 'for the sick feel as shamed as the sinful, as fallen' I knew exactly what he meant—although I now know that that place of physical shame is open to anyone: it takes less than a heartbeat to travel there, claim residence.

It matters because the act of speaking about pain feels almost unbearably impossible. It matters because it outright hurts to write. It seems to me that human hurt might be one of the core reasons why language came into existence in the first place—underneath the intricate system of dictionary, after all, is the scream, the raw instinctive impulse to sound out what pains, what endangers us, to pull help close, to warn other animals away. It seems likely to me that when the word first graced the hard ground we walked, it burst from our primal cries, it flowed from our wounds, it pulsed from our shudders and our hardships, it formed around our needs and aches. It was physical, made of flesh from the outset, spoke what mattered to the body, what was crucial to survival.

We may find ourselves combating what Scarry calls pain's implicit 'shattering of language', reduced once again to that primitive state of shaping little more on the page than a gut-wrenched groan, but we have to take up the challenge, as Virginia Woolf describes it, of smashing our pain out of silence, into audibility, 'tak[ing our] pain in one hand and a lump of pure sound in the other, so to crush them together that a brand new word drops out'. It matters that we find new shards of language that can talk raw hurt, that can let pain be faced, and known, and spoken. It might be a jagged pathography, it might have to scalpel away layers of shame, crack old narrative models into skeletal fragments, but it's necessary surgery, for many of us desperately so.

It matters that when students arrive in my classroom, and they do, who have been to this other place, I can look them in the face and say, 'Write it. It counts. Your words will be listened to.' What I remember most from that place on the ward, other than the pain, is the terrible echo of its distances, the stretch of empty impassable miles between the outpost of each bed, the far-off grid of windows a barred horizon on a world so remote it no longer exists. It matters that those of us who lay in that place find a way to reach across those distances, that we try to send some link, some signal to one another, even if all we can do is trade whispers, chant desolations, offer words that are little more than wails, witness the sad community of those who find themselves, as Hilary Mantel terms it, 'down there with the animals'. That might be all we can do.

*

So I have no triumphant ending to round off this essay. All I can leave you with is one of the slender threads I found that first helped me trace my way back. Because I did come home, piece by slow piece, in and out of endless days, across

years, in pain, to writing. And one of the first things I found myself writing
was a story, commissioned by a strange blessed twist from one of Katherine
Mansfield's last unfinished fragments. Of course, when faced with this project,
fresh from the hospital, all I could think of was her illness, the fate she shared
with so many others of her era, immured in sanatoriums: in my imagination
Mansfield's sickened body was wheeled into place as indelibly as the woman
who lay beside me on the ward, breath scraping through her battered chest.
So I started some research into Mansfield's world of pain, into the cut-off
realms of the consumptive, into the gothic and snowbound enclosures where
the dispossessed of this disease were stored. Out on the porches where the
beds were wheeled to heal in the freezing alpine air, my character stared at the
soundless far-gone faces around her in sub-zero rows:

*Thin as salt, the snow litters our blankets, hardens to a slate. We could scratch our
names on it. But we don't. Perhaps this is despair. But that seems too active, too
strenuous a word, too much like a call that still expects to be answered. A cry that
imagines it could be consoled. Instead, it is zero, zero that the open eyes show; it is
nothing that gapes in the faces. The woman beside me cries, motionless. Her eyes
release a long, fused series of tears. They are incidental and soon frozen. Body by
body we are dyed white, whiter, in our steel groves. Below, above, there are storeys
of us. Ice stretches a ghetto from face to face.*

But I also discovered that the children of the tuberculosis wards, who were
often tied into their beds, would sometimes, against all odds, slip loose, and
stealthily unhook each other, and would use their cords to bind up tiny trails
of notes that they'd scratch down and suspend out the windows of their wing.
The image of those tremors of paper, signals smudged by brave child fingers to
anyone beyond the prison who might listen, testified to the fact that sending
out even the frailest string of words represents hope, that the impulse to reach
for one another with the thinnest scraps of ink persists in us, is in itself near
unkillable. Even in pain we want to be seen, we want to be heard, we want to be
found. That image, those dangling strips of paper, continued to flicker within
my mind with the message that somehow writing will always matter.

REFERENCES

Everyone who is born … Susan Sontag, *Illness as Metaphor and Aids and Its Metaphors* (London: Penguin, 1991), p. 1.

the common world of the uninjured … W.H. Auden, *Selected Poetry of W.H. Auden* (New York: Vintage, 1971), p. 45.

the army of the upright … Virginia Woolf, 'On Being Ill', in *The Essays of Virginia Woolf: Volume 5, 1929 to 1932* (London: Hogarth Press, 2009), p. 198.

Physical pain, as Elaine Scarry reminds us … Elaine Scarry, *The Body in Pain* (Oxford: Oxford University Press, 1985).

Let a sufferer try to explain …; when the lights of health go down …; undiscovered country … Woolf, 'On Being Ill'.

for the sick feel as shamed … John Updike, 'The City', in *Trust Me: Stories* (London: Penguin, 1987), p. 35.

shattering of language … Scarry, *The Body in Pain*, p. 5.

tak[ing our] pain in one hand … Woolf, 'On Being Ill', p. 196.

down there with the animals … Hilary Mantel, *Giving up the Ghost: A memoir* (London: Harper Perennial, 2003), p. 208.

TIM UPPERTON

A Lifted Stone

Much is hidden from us. Behind the smooth painted and plastered lining of
the walls of my living room, where I sit and write, less than a metre away from
me creatures are stirring, and have their secret life. Sometimes I hear the dry
scuttle of a mouse, but other, smaller creatures—woodlice, whitetail spiders,
click beetles, ants—these creatures are silent and seldom reveal themselves.
Occasionally I notice a daddy-long-legs swaying slightly in a corner of the
ceiling, or a solitary chocolate-coloured cockroach spreadeagled on the wall,
stunned by the light as I trudge to the bathroom in the early hours. The borer
chews a hole in the skirting board, with only a little brown dust to show for its
industry. I imagine it deep in the wood, nestled like a rabbit in its burrow, its
scrap of life ticking.

When I was a child I was obsessed with the hidden life that went about its
business all around me, I had to see it, had to know it. I would carefully remove
the pale pupating huhu grubs that lay buried in rotting stumps like pharaohs
in their tombs, and keep them in jars of damp sawdust until they emerged as
winged beetles, still white and frail-looking, their long antennae testing the
air. I would turn over planks of wood to see what lived under them: brown
beetles, black soft-bellied spiders with white egg-sacs, grey hump-backed slugs,
orange slimy flatworms. I discovered tiny transparent balls that I thought were
snails' eggs, and I preserved them in purple methylated spirits in little labelled
bottles sealed with corks. At the windswept beach where my family camped
each summer I would crouch on the reef at low tide, the sea a distant, uneven
roar, like traffic, and I would lift the weed-encrusted stones in the rockpools
to expose the creatures that teemed underneath. The almost invisible glassy
shrimps would dart backwards. The brown cockabullies would flash past the
cautiously retreating hermit crabs. The anemones would wave their thin arms
among the inert kina and cushion starfish. It seemed very strange to me that all

these creatures coexisted under the stone, as in a darkened house, in a kind of dormancy, until I lifted the roof and the blazing light fell upon them.

Years later, as a young man, I worked as a librarian at a polytechnic in Dartford, Kent. To get to Dartford—a grey, industrial satellite town southeast of London, built over what used to be apple orchards—I had to get up very early in the morning at my flat in Golders Green, a suburb in the northwest of the city, and travel for two hours by bus, tube, British Rail and finally a shuttle, sometimes above ground, sometimes below, mostly in darkness. The train would hurtle along past indistinct office buildings and warehouses, into a tunnel and then out into the open air, past grimy factories and apartment blocks built right beside the railway line. In some apartments, lit windows, bright yellow rectangles, appeared like frames in an incoherent film: now, a kitchen, with a young child holding a red plastic toy and standing beside the fridge, reaching up to an adult just out of view; now, a bathroom with what looked like a white bottle of some kind—shampoo?—on the window ledge, the window clouded with steam; now, a living room; now, an empty, different kitchen with the blue-yellow glow of a gas fire.

I remember, revealed in one of those yellow rectangles, a man about my own age in a white, unbuttoned business shirt, shaving briskly in the mirror, his chin and jowls all lathered up; in another, an older woman in a blue dressing-gown brushing her long grey hair. There was something about the domestic ordinariness of these glimpses into other lives that made them vivid; I wondered about the man, and the woman, about the circumstances of their lives, and where their lives would take them. The rails brought us momentarily into proximity and then made distance between us again, and they continued along their ways, that I knew nothing of, and I continued along mine, each of us bound somewhere. They were unaware, but they must have heard the passing train, and if they had looked out they would perhaps have seen a pale face at a window of the train, for a moment, and then gone.

Now, as I turn on the tap to fill the kettle, I hear a gurgling in the plumbing and I remember that the water supply has been turned off at the street for some hours as contractors are digging a trench for the installation of fibre-optic cable. The cable—really many cables bundled together, each insulated in bright blue sheathing—lies along the grass berm, but soon it will be buried and I will never see it again. Beneath the ground it will ferry data at unbelievable speed between my computer and the world beyond. The water is back on, and in a sort of convulsion it bursts from the tap, orange with rust, and flecked with clots of green-black algae. And these have always been there, inside the pipe that leads to the tap—if I look closely I can see a rind of green at the spout, surviving despite the chlorine-treated water that rushes through it every day. The outside of the tap is gleaming chrome but this belies what it is like inside, where no light shines, where rust collects and algae grows.

I am a poor housekeeper, and I don't notice the dust, the food crumbs, the detritus that accumulates daily, like a thickening skin, in the living areas of my home—over the piano that no one plays, the framed photos on top of the piano, the dining table, the benches, the bookcases. Dead flies multiply on the windowsills. Then a friend is coming to visit, or my older children are coming home for the weekend, and I am suddenly ashamed, and launch into a frenzy of cleaning. It is now I find things long forgotten, lost and rediscovered—a book I thought someone had borrowed; unused postage stamps on a high shelf; letters from my mother, who died five years ago, full of news about her garden and earnestly enquiring about my health.

Recently I resolved to change all this, and to begin living in a cleaner, more orderly fashion. I began with the bookshelf nearest to me, and to clean it properly I pulled out the books—cheap hardbound editions of Dickens, each with a thin layer of grey dust along its top. I wiped them with a damp cloth and checked them for mildew, and I thought about how long it had been since I had read them. I'd bought these books as a bulk lot at a garage sale over thirty years ago, when I was an undergraduate. I sometimes take down my favourites— *David Copperfield*, *Little Dorrit*, *Our Mutual Friend*—but others I have never read, or barely started. *A Tale of Two Cities*: what's that about? 'It was the best of times, it was the worst of times …' Everyone knows the beginning, but then what? What happens? How does it end? I don't know. And Edwin Drood— isn't he murdered? Who kills him? Or does he merely disappear, to come back triumphantly at the end? I don't know. Dickens died with the novel unfinished, so maybe he didn't know either.

One of the most memorable characters in *David Copperfield* is Rosa Dartle, who has been toyed with and discarded by the caddish Steerforth. She talks always in an insinuating manner, putting others on edge with her questions. Her constant disingenuous refrain is that she only wants to know, that she cares only for information. It's not true, or not the whole truth, but it speaks to me, that desire to know. I read *The Pickwick Papers* for the first time not so long ago, but already details are becoming hazy, characters half forgotten or merged with other characters. Alfred Jingle, Sam Weller—I remember them, but I would need to read the book again to get it all straight in my mind. And for a couple of years now it's been closed on the shelf, its pages pressed together, the Phiz illustrations hard against lines of cramped text on the opposing page, the text itself meaningless and indecipherable until I crack it open again.

Beneath the volumes of Dickens I have a couple of shelves of nineteenth-century Russian novels, from the same garage sale, Turgenev and Dostoyevsky and Pushkin and Tolstoy, most of them unread, except Tolstoy. They just sit there. But I can open *Anna Karenina* and suddenly there she is, Anna, flirting with Vronsky, the two of them conversing – then just as suddenly silent again as I clap the book shut.

For my tenth birthday I asked my parents to get me the enormous *Larousse Encyclopaedia of Animal Life*. I still have it, in its torn glossy dustjacket. It's followed me through my adolescence and then my twenties, into marriage and out again, through a dozen houses, fatherhood and jobs; sometimes for years it has sat in a storage box. For most of my life it's been there. I remember my anticipation as I tore off the wrapping and first exposed its solid mass, just waiting to be opened, consumed. It began with protozoa, single-celled organisms, and progressed up the evolutionary chain, ending with the primates, with us. I had this crazy idea—that I would copy out the entire text, and reproduce the pictures, and that as I did so, all the information the encyclopaedia contained would be absorbed into me, and I would know all there was to know about animals. And so I set to my task, but I never got any further than the protozoa. I quickly realised that my ambition outstripped my enthusiasm, and that there would be things about animals that I would never know. But I took comfort from the fact that, if I needed to know something, I could look it up in the book. The encyclopaedia was like a giant brain, an oracle. I could ask it whatever I needed to know and it would give me the answer.

It seemed to me, when I was a child, that I knew very little and my parents knew everything. When I had to take some foul-tasting medicine as I recovered from a tonsillectomy I resorted to hiding the medicine bottle in the pocket of my raincoat, which was hanging in my wardrobe. 'Where have you put it?' my mother asked. She looked at me shrewdly. She knew I had hidden it. Then she walked directly to my wardrobe, flung it open, and reached into my raincoat pocket. She knew. I was helpless in the face of this absolute knowledge. 'Poke out your tongue,' she would say. 'If you are lying, there will be an L on your tongue.' I would close my mouth tight, and of course she would know I was lying anyway. As I grew older, I came to realise her knowledge was not absolute after all. When she asked if it had been me who scratched 'Zorro' on the front panel of the oak sideboard I denied it, I cried, and shook my head, and she believed me. I was one of many children, and it struck me in that moment that although she might suspect, she could not know it was me—and so, even though I had done it, it was wrong to punish me, as only I knew in my heart that I was guilty. And how could she know what was in my heart?

Now it seems to me that we can never know what is in anybody's heart. We can infer some things from how a person behaves—a giveaway tremor, a tell-tale gesture—or from what someone says and the tone in which it is said. But we cannot know for sure. There is an L on every tongue. If sincerity is to be inferred from the sum of our gestures and our speech, then the best actor, the most plausible liar, is the most sincere person of all. Despite this, observation of external details is the only way we have of knowing other people, because we are not privy to their inner thoughts and feelings. I may know, for example, that a man is pretentious and vain, or that a woman is flirting with a man she has just met at a party. I know these things from observing their outward behaviour. They, in turn, may know all sorts of things about me from my outward behaviour.

Such knowledge is provisional, unscientific and prone to error, but it is the only kind of knowledge of each other that is available to us. Our inner motives, our feelings, the emotional currents that push us to and fro are hidden from view, not just from others, but even from ourselves. What seemed clear to Descartes— that he could catch himself in the act of thinking and inspect his own mind—is today considered naïve. In the great nineteenth-century novels, in *Pride and Prejudice* and *Middlemarch* and *The Bostonians* and *War and Peace* and so on, as we listen to the cool, ironic voice of the narrator or the author, we have a comforting sense of someone who knows these characters inside out, even if the characters don't know themselves very well.

At the same time, we understand that this omniscience is an illusion. Modernism and, in particular, the modern science of psychology, have put paid to all that. The totalising tendencies of the old novels are, we know, now out of date, made obsolete by the discoveries of Jung and Freud, and at odds with the way life is actually experienced. The narrative strategies in the stories of Katherine Mansfield, or the novels of D.H. Lawrence or Virginia Woolf, are fundamentally different, and their modernist representations of character are different too, even from those in the fiction of their slightly older contemporaries, such as H.G. Wells and John Galsworthy and Arnold Bennett. 'On or about December 1910, human character changed,' Woolf says in her essay on the subject, 'Mr Bennett and Mrs Brown', and so it did, though her phrasing is a warning not to take dates too seriously. That is, our concept of human character changed to accommodate developing ideas about the subconscious and especially the unconscious, the unknown countries of the mind. Our desire to enter these unexplored regions, to map their topography and describe their unique features, must necessarily fail. The salient point about the unconscious is that we are not conscious of it; to drag it into the light is to transform it into a simulacrum of itself, like pinning a butterfly to a board. To accept this necessary failure is to accept that what is hidden must sometimes remain so, to accept mysteriousness—the mysteriousness of others and of ourselves.

This acceptance is not comfortable, and probably impossible as a permanent state of mind. I work from home, and the nature of my work is such that I can go for days at a time without seeing or communicating directly with others, apart from my immediate family. Then I go out to buy groceries, or to a movie, and I'm astonished by how much certitude there is everywhere—the confident tone in which strangers address each other and make various transactions, the loud laughter, the way people stride along without looking left or right. Perhaps I present this same confidence to others, even as I feel, sometimes, that I'm navigating my way through a fog of anxiety down vertiginous streets, even as I feel like a complete fool. But, I say to myself, we are all fools in the world.

My eldest child, an adult now, writes poetry. His poems are sometimes

enigmatic, they evoke a feeling, a mood, but I don't always understand them.
I want to, perhaps out of a desire to understand him. It's as if the poems might
reveal to me something about him that is hidden, as if they are a stone that
might be lifted. But it's no good me asking what a particular line means. He just
shrugs and grins. We both know the strangeness of poetry, the impossibility of
paraphrase—it's what makes us come back to read the same short poem again.
There it is, the poem, on the white page with nowhere to hide, yet concealing
some of itself. And this is true of all the poems I love most. I memorise these
poems, to take them into myself, just as I laboriously drew copies of protozoa
all those years ago, and with the same frustration, the knowledge of their being
beyond my grasp. They feel a part of me, just as my liver and kidneys and heart
are parts of me, hidden inside my body, working in ways I don't understand to
help me live.

Two poets I read over and over, Paul Celan and Wallace Stevens, I understand
hardly at all. I can say nothing about Celan, I understand him so little, and as I
speak no German I read him only in translation—and poetry, they say, is what
is lost in translation. With Stevens I am on more familiar ground but again I feel
like a fool. Who, in his 'Thirteen Ways of Looking at a Blackbird', are the 'thin
men of Haddam'?

> O thin men of Haddam,
> Why do you imagine golden birds?
> Do you not see how the blackbird
> Walks around the feet
> Of the women about you?

Haddam, Google tells me, is a small town in Connecticut (there is another
Haddam in Kansas but I don't think Stevens meant that one). Stevens' tone is
gently chastising, like that of Jesus talking to his disciples. I have read exegeses of
this line—that it alludes to Eliot's hollow men, for example—but these explana-
tions take me away from the poem, when what I want is to get nearer. They don't
help. And what is the meaning of the anecdote in 'Anecdote of the Jar'?

> I placed a jar in Tennessee,
> And round it was, upon a hill.
> It made the slovenly wilderness
> Surround that hill.

It's not even an anecdote. I've heard it suggested that the jar is an analogue for Keats' urn—again, no help. But these poems fascinate me, I love them in a deeper way than those I also love but understand better, such as Elizabeth Bishop's 'One Art', a poem I often teach to poetry-writing students. It's easy to demonstrate how Bishop's villanelle structure is ideally suited to her theme of accumulating losses, and to show the poem's rhetorical failure that is also its success. 'The art of losing isn't hard to master,' Bishop says again and again, and each time we believe her a little less. Some losses cannot be mastered, cannot be borne. I love the poem, and I know it by heart, but I can see all around it. I feel that it is wholly revealed to me, finished, whereas Celan and Stevens and even my own son hide things from me. I am drawn to the unknown, to the mystery. What is the known, compared with this? A lighted window, a lifted stone.

The book of literary criticism I return to most is William Empson's *Seven Types of Ambiguity*, first published in 1930, much of it written while Empson was still an undergraduate at Cambridge. Empson's subtle analysis of ambiguity in poetry begins with metaphor, where two apparently unlike things are identified, and ends with the most extreme type of ambiguity, where a word has two opposite meanings, and both meanings are entertained in the context of the poem. One of Empson's extreme examples is drawn from Gerard Manley Hopkins' sonnet 'The Windhover'. Hopkins admires the physical splendour of the eponymous bird, but he also recognises that, as a Jesuit priest, a follower of Christ, his spiritual values are at odds with this admiration: it represents, to him, a lack of humility. This mental conflict is manifested in the language of the poem: 'Brute beauty and valour and act, oh, air, pride, plume, here/ Buckle!' Empson observes that 'Buckle!' can mean to join together in strength, as in the buckling of a military belt, but it can also mean to weaken and collapse, as in the buckling of a bicycle wheel. The conflict in Hopkins' mind is thus encapsulated neatly in a contronym.

Such analysis is illuminating, and ingenious, but it doesn't account for the most significant thing about Hopkins, the thing that must strike every reader who encounters him for the first time, which is his singular weirdness. Sometimes I would like a friend, or even a literary critic, anyone, just to point at a poem and say, in wonder, 'Look at this. Isn't it weird? See how weird it is.' Sometimes that would be enough. Instead of shining a light fiercely on the poem, we would see by its own light into the surrounding dark. And we would look at the poem together for a while, abiding in its weirdness, warming ourselves at its fire.

#Mothersday

It is the day before Mother's Day. We are celebrating early and, despite Mum's alcohol addiction, we will do so with cold cider.

I used to give her disapproving looks when I saw her tea cup filled with cold drinks that were not tea. These days, however, I'm more likely to swallow judgement.

I'm tolerating the excuses she makes: her pains—arthritic, memories of childhood scoliosis, so much stuff, so deep and metastasised. I still roll my eyes often enough. You can't fix that shit with alcohol, Mum; alcohol won't stop your joints from swelling, it'll swell them more; won't stop your back from crooking, it'll crook more; won't stop all the people you love and miss from being dead … But I have to stop there. I can't say it'll make the people she lost deader. Dead is dead. And Leonard Cohen's not helping either.

Mum's flat is like an op shop—the lovely kind. At first glance it promises quarter-century-old daisies pressed into shelved books, a real ruby somewhere, maybe a moa feather. I say, 'God, Mum. Seriously. Let something go.'

But I'm stealing looks at things, faces.

We'll celebrate Mother's Day with a drink.

Mum deserves a daughter who accepts her just the way she is. Had alcohol been the cause of a horrid childhood, it'd be harder to make that call or pour the booze. But it didn't. I remember as a kid coming home from school once to discover my bed wasn't made and the house wasn't steamed up from the meat and three vege cooking well before the 5-o'clock-on-the-dot dinner time. The day I arrived to this—the unmade bed and no dinner—I figured someone else was dead. And I hoped it wouldn't be another person the same age as me. When I found Mum in the kitchen, not crying and without terrible news to tell, I said, 'Mum, what's happened?'

Mum always had everything just-so, freshly this, crisply that, and she could mostly always be found at home. If not, she returned with something to make sure we knew we'd been thought of while she was gone. I most often got paper, pencils or books. After Glen Bo died that was one of the first things I was given—a blank book, with just some words in dark calligraphy on the first page:

In memory of Glen Bo Duggan
1983–1994

The book was to help me get through. To process. I could write about him, Mum said. Poems, memories—anything I liked. The book got me away from smashing the dead tree at the back of our farm with an axe. Mum believed I could write it out, that was one of the best things she believed in. Me, and that I would—could—write.

Let's go for a walk. I want to take you somewhere. Before we do, I'll tell you this: in high school I was nicknamed Sad Girl. And that's not another story.

Let's walk to the first of three trees. The first was a large willow at the back of our farm. Climbing it brought you above the chicken house. It brought you above a tin shed. It brought you above the rest of the world, really.

Glen Bo, Kodie and I used to climb it. We used to climb into the branches to play. I remember Glen and I pretending it was our house, and we'd sit up there looking out at the rest of the world and drink imaginary tea together. Until Mum called us for 5-o'clock-on-the-dot dinner. Then we would climb down. That was before, though—before Glen Bo left. He went to go and live with his mum again—which I could never understand. Wasn't he happy with us, climbing trees until dinner? Sometimes we fished, sometimes we rode bikes, sometimes we go-carted. We got 5-o'clock-on-the-dot dinners, beds made, eggs from chooks. We lay by the fire, played at the beach. Wasn't it good? It was, he said, but every boy wants his mother, no matter. His dad was already dead.

Mum told us he would still be able to come for holidays, and he did. Once. Once before his stepfather beat him with a hearth brush.

When Glen Bo lay in a hospital bed in Christchurch and me and Kodie were in Birchfield being looked after by our older sister because Mum was at Glen Bo's bedside, Tami didn't quite manage the 5-o'clock-on-the-dot dinners. They were good—but not predictable. They were nourishing—but didn't cater to a gnawing emotional need for everything to stay the same, adventure to be tempered with predictability. They didn't assure us no one would get hurt beyond what a plaster, worst-case scenario some stitches or a cast, could fix. And I went out and stood under the tree that me and Glen Bo had climbed together and made a promise: I would not go sit on our special branch until he got better.

'I won't, Glen,' I said.

But he didn't. He died instead. And he wore a cap in his little coffin so we didn't have to look at the scars that scissored across his shaven head. Which, apart from his not breathing, told us that what had happened to him could not be fixed with plasters. Or stitches. Or casts. You can't stitch, plaster or cast a bruised brain.

Nor a broken heart, we found.

And I did look. I lifted the cap and touched his scar. A scar you might expect from falling hard from a tall, tall tree. At that time I had no real understanding at all of why he was dead. I looked at him and hoped to see him move. Hoped to see him sit up—I willed it with all the rest of my life's birthday wishes and all of my heart. And so often I thought I had brought him back to life, thought I saw him try to open his eyes.

'Did you see that?' I would say to myself. 'He tried to wake up.'

I believed in more things then. Miracles and imaginary tea and that when 5 o'clock came around, everyone would come to the table.

There's another tree, though. Let's go there. It will help us feel better.

In the same paddock as the one we climbed together was a fallen one. Mum gave me an axe and I was allowed to smash that tree. And that became all I did after school each day. I would come home, pick up my axe, go out to the back of the farm and smash that dead tree. Pretend it was something, someone else.

But come now. This is too much violence. Come to a third tree, on another farm. One day my friends and I walked there and lay beneath it to talk. I looked up through the branches to the fractured light and realised that I was carrying on. I had not climbed into Glen's casket and been buried with him. Our family had buried something, though—and not just Glen Bo. Something else went with him we would never get back.

I lay with my head resting on a tree root and felt—for the first time since Glen Bo died—that I was happy. But by then something in my face had changed. Something in my eyes. Though I lifted my head from the root I rested on and walked home feeling happy to be on my way to my 5-o'clock-on-the-dot dinner, I was already Sad Girl.

Don't talk like that back in Mum's flat, though. At least I won't.

Me and Mum are heading out because I have a surprise for Mum and she's going to love it.

You see, I entered something I wrote into a Short Story Competition. I entered it especially because I wanted Catherine Chidgey to read it. (Not for weird reasons, just because I respect her opinion, and if she deemed my short story the best then I'd believe her.) She is the Judge of the Short Story Competition. She was only going to read the top ten, and I don't know who was to choose the top ten, but that's okay because no doubt my story is somewhere in there.

My mum has always been my biggest fan. She loves everything I write. I'm not going to say she is my *only* fan, because that would sound like self-deprecation, which is a most pathetic way to draw attention to yourself. Plus Mum hates it. Self-deprecation, I mean.

So we head out. First stop: a drink and a bite to eat at The Vic on Trafalgar Street. Yes, we have a drink, and yes, we clink our drinks, and it's not awkward. After eating we head to the place where they will announce the winners of the Short Story Competition.

Mum doesn't know why we are at this place, where they have closed the doors and put out trays of quartered club sandwiches and OJ on a small table. I haven't told her why we are here; I just said writers might read and it could be fun.

I want to surprise her.

It is cool that poet—and my former writing tutor—Cliff Fell is a guest speaker. He makes a beautiful presentation about death and poetry, and how art is the real meaning of life. Both Mum and I appreciate everything he says.

When it comes time for an official to announce the winners my heart beats faster. All Mum's work and support has finally paid off. Surprise! Happy Mother's Day, I'll say. And she will be at a loss. A happy, proud loss.

A woman begins reading the list of winners. By the time she gets to the top five, I think: 'Shit, I must be right up there!' As place four and three are read my heart pounds, because wow, my name must be getting close. Final two. And no,

I am not in second and now there is only first left, this is going to be the best day ever. Mum is going to be so happy!

The woman reads the winner's name and it blurs into the sound of my heart pumping not-a-winner's blood through my not-a-winner's body.

I clap, smile. Mum does too.

'You should have entered. You would have won,' Mum says.

I smile. 'I did enter.'

'Oh,' she says. 'Oh, Becky Boo.'

We leave without having a club sandwich. We wander back down Trafalgar Street. To shop, have dinner and go to a movie.

'This is the worst day,' I say, and we laugh.

I start telling Mum about my hopes of winning.

'When I hadn't heard my name by second place I was thinking, shit, Mum's going to love this!'

We get hysterical, we look like drunk fools, laughing and laughing till we double over trying to walk back down Trafalgar Street, prize-less. 'Oh Becky Boo,' Mum laughs.

'I wanted to take you to the bookshop and buy you books with the vouchers I would have won,' I say.

'Your story was probably too good,' Mum says.

'Yeah.'

We are forced to spend our own money shopping rather than the winner's prize vouchers for Page and Blackmore's bookshop. Mum is out of foundation and needs a hair dye so we go to Farmers instead. In front of Farmers there is a monk peddling happiness in the form of a book, which one can have upon a small donation.

'No one has cash any more, we have cards!' Mum smiles.

The monk whips a portable Eftpos machine from his pocket.

Mum and I pretend not to see it and rummage in our purses for change. We both find more than we thought we had.

The monk opens his front-facing fanny-pack. Mum tries to deposit her donation in it but becomes confused. 'Is it in?' she asks, holding the change in a fist at the monk's crotch, lest it tinkle upon the pavement. 'Have I got it yet?' Her hand lingers at his crotch for a super-weird amount of time. I stifle a giggle. This is awkward. Almost as awkward as waiting to be announced the winner of the Short Story Competition and leaving a non-winner who doesn't congratulate the actual winners who bothered to show.

We go into Farmers. 'They should wear those things to the side,' Mum says.

'I think they will from now on.'

We crack up laughing. We crack up laughing hard-out.

*

1994 seems so long ago.

We had a lot to contend with then. Children are quite resilient, though: I was already something like happy a few months after Glen Bo's funeral, and then I found ten-month-old J drowned in a bucket of water and was reminded that coffins come in all shapes and sizes. Like hooks and lines and sinkers.

Our family is brought to balance by its few stoic men. Mostly fishermen, who all have gumboots stained with guts, and more than one scar each from spikes, knives, shiny hooks.

I think that's why I hate that I screamed. That's why when Dad pulled up beside me, walking down the gravelly road in Waimangaroa—not caring for my bare feet, my forgotten shoes—I just got in the car and said nothing. I'd been with my friend Jodi, and Mrs M answered the door when we knocked.

She had said, 'He was just out of my sight for a minute.'

And either I, or Jodi, said, 'Don't worry, Mrs M, we'll help you look.'

And she said, 'Just a minute.'

And we said, 'Naughty baby.'

I took off my shoes and we went inside Mrs M's house and as we did I noticed that her hands were splayed. We giggled as we looked under the bed and as we sang: 'Come out, come out, wherever you are …'

I saw that the laundry door was open a crack. I pushed it and when I saw legs sticking up from the big bucket I turned to a sand-bag.

I looked away and Mrs M caught my eye and it was then that I screamed. Not right after I found him, but when I saw her find in my face that I had found him.

Found her naughty baby.

I left, forgetting my shoes. There was no sound of sirens. Not yet. Not out here in the whops. Dad pulled up, though, and I couldn't tell him what had happened. I just got in the back of the car like I'd been barefoot at the beach.

The local policeman came to see me and Mum. His name was Garry Southon and he brought me a stuffed toy lion.

'For being very brave.'

As I took it to my room I think I heard him tell Mum that there had been a spoon in the water, and J must have wanted it because it was so shiny. I think that's what I heard, but I never asked anyone so I can't be sure.

Mum and I went to visit J's family and Mrs M was lovely to me and hugged me and said look, he is so beautiful, so peaceful, an angel. Now I know she must have been pumped up to her eyeballs with Valium or something to help her accept that her baby was dead. When I arrived at the house I discovered that one of J's sisters was mad at me for having screamed when I found him. She and her friends sat on the bed listening to Eric Clapton singing 'Tears in Heaven' and I felt like an outsider who had looked at something I shouldn't have, like my finding J dead was the reason he was dead. But Mrs M hugged me. And I was okay cause J wasn't mine to feel sad about. I didn't love J. I loved Glen Bo, so I knew that this was not my pain, this was theirs. For them I could only feel sorry, and deep, childlike indignation.

*

Mum has found the right hair dye. 'This has been the worst day,' I say. Even though we know that isn't even nearly true.

'It has been the best-ever worst day, Becky Boo.'

Mum and Dad raised four very different people. Kodie, the youngest, is as stoic and predictable as an old man on the sea.

Tami mothers like a lioness but is sensitive. Meanwhile Nicole abandoned her children, joined the Mongrel Mob, married a man named Katdog, and I have hardly spoken to her since.

Sometimes I am a normal person—a happy, responsible normal person. Sometimes I miss the family we were. I miss Nicole, even. Wish my kids could call her Aunty Nic. Then again, fuck her and her Sieg fucken heil. Deserter.

'Have you heard from Nicole?' I ask Mum.

Mum's heard rumours, sometimes straight from Nicole. That he beats her, that he doesn't beat her, that she calls him by his real name now, that he beats her, that he doesn't—or at least not any more.

As Mum speaks, I feel a deep ache to have my sister back. For Mum to go to the kitchen and make lasagne. For us to sit down and have kai together again.

I don't know how it would feel to know your daughter was being beaten. Your own child. The baby you brought into this world.

*

Glen Bo came to live with us partly because his father was dead. Uncle Terry was found in his car outside his home on 31 July 1991. He died of respiratory failure consistent with narcotic or sedative drug overdose. And before he died of a drug overdose Uncle Glen had died of a drug overdose, and now Mum is an alcoholic and the very best I can do to help is pour her less drink than I would a non-alcoholic. I never say, drink up, let's get wasted, like I might to a non-alcoholic like myself.

But who am I kidding? Mum is a better person than me, straight up. Her worst trait is that she cares about every single person alive, and if you care about every single person alive, and most of them are suffering, you are going to need a drink.

Glen Bo's mother came up to me after his funeral and gave me his copy of Tolkien's *Lord of the Rings*. I thought that was lovely of her. It was probably hard for her to know how to grieve, considering how much she must have blamed herself for own son's death. She had got herself cleaned up and was rewarded with getting Glen Bo back. No longer using? Sure, have your beautiful little boy back.

But she did use again. In fact on 14 April 1994, less than a month before Mother's Day, she was in rehab and Glen Bo had been left with his stepfather, Peter Wayne Ryder, who beat him over a period of two days, eventually putting him in a coma from which he would never wake. His life support was turned off on 18 April. Mum called Tami and Tami had to tell us and all we did was cry and cry and want Mum home right now. Glen Bo home, Mum home. Bring Glen Bo. Five-o'clock-on-the-dot.

We don't know where Glen Bo's mum is now.

'I just can't understand why she didn't call me. He could have come back to us,' Mum has said. Often.

She must have known Peter shouldn't care for her son alone. He must have been violent before. To her, to him. Must have.

The scar tissue from using needles, I reckon, is worse than what is visible. The scar tissue must run to bone, making everything silken and gummy. Even your spine.

*

It's almost time to get to the movie.

Mum walks really slowly.

I think about Mrs M losing J, I think about Glen Bo's mum, I think about Tami and Nicole. I wonder if the next time I am with all my siblings together in one room it will be at Mum's funeral. I shouldn't be thinking about Mum's funeral because here she is walking with me, but I can't help it because she brings it up. I sometimes say, 'Look at all this stuff you have in this tiny flat!' And she says, 'When I'm dead you can get rid of it all.'

'But look, you must be happy I kept this,' she'll say, holding a shell. I bought it for her from an op shop for 10 cents when I was about nine years old. I had gone in with 10 cents. I found a jar that had buttons and shells and other tiny things inside and the jar had a label saying that the items in it cost 20 cents each, but I told the shop owner I only had 10 cents, could I choose one for just 10 cents? And she said yes I could, so I chose a small polished shell and I took it home and wrapped it up and gave it to Mum for either her birthday or Mother's Day, I can't remember which.

After that I remember going to another shop with Mum, I think it was DEKA, and I found a toy I wanted and I told Mum I didn't have enough, but it would be okay because when I bought the shell for you, Mum, they didn't mind that I didn't have enough money. She laughed loud and told me this was is a normal shop, not an op shop. You have to stick to the price. When I look back at that I am so surprised that I couldn't see the difference. Sure the light was brighter in DEKA, and the floor cleaner. But couldn't a kid shake her pocket money out on the counter and be forgiven a dollar's discrepancy?

As a kid I thought mountains looked like giants—nice giants like the BFG that had been lying there so long, so quiet and calm that grass and trees had just grown over them. They were not dead, but lying there under a green blanket hoping children would come along and picnic on their knees and noses and steal giant pennies from their pockets so they'd have something to laugh at.

But they were actually just mountains.

Normal mountains, so stick to the price, black and white, and don't give me a dollar less than you owe.

Glen Bo might have snuck $5 from Peter Wayne Ryder's wallet. And Peter demanded it back. Glen Bo couldn't explain where the money was, so he was beaten. Beaten to death. I reckon if he took that fiver at all, he would have spent it on lollies to share with his buddies, or polished shells from an op shop for his mother.

*

It is already five o'clock when we order what is only our second drink for the day at Stefano's Pizzeria—but we have had a ball. We have our tickets to watch *Tully*, which I thought was based on a book I read as a teen but isn't.

The tickets cost $33, and we accept the proper prices and normal names for things, and you never learn much about anyone unless you walk somewhere with them.

So thank you.

'Mum, let's get a selfie.'

'Okay,' Mum says. 'Don't get my double chin.'

I post the one Mum likes best on Facebook.

I write: This lady #MothersDay.

And that is all you should have seen, really. The selfie Mum chose. Not her flat, nor what is really in her tea cup, nor the crook of her spine.

Not what killed her brothers or the guilt she feels for Glen Bo.

Just how beautiful she is.

Loess

If you were to fly like a crow from Dunedin to Wanaka you would pass over a brown lumpy landscape before you reached the mountainous mountains and the lakes of Central Otago proper. This is a block and basin, or basin and range, or horst and something landscape. The ranges, blocks, horsts are clearly defined raised heaps caused by geological uplift and tilted so that one face is steep and the other gentle. Over millennia the basins in between have filled up with all the stuff basins fill up with, and erosion has exposed the schist into a fretted landscape with great jutting tors. It has the most extreme climate in New Zealand—parched hot in summer and sub-zero in winter.

Some think these exposed flat-topped blocks—the Rock and Pillar, Rough Ridge, Lammerlaws, Lammermoors, Hawkduns—are only good for farming wind. The Rock and Pillar is especially remarkable for the forcefulness and abundance of its wind. It is a womb of wind and cloud and begets its own particular lenticular cloud formation, 'The Taieri Pet', which can loom large overhead like a great Aeolian spaceship.

Everything is blown, and every dip and gap and crevice is filled with loess, a wind-blown mix of fine silt and clay and ash, blasted into the cracks in the tors, whisked into the gullies, swamped in the bogs, and becoming ground for plants to take root and insects to make burrows.

The wind strikes the high schist tors, funnelling around at an increased speed so that in winter, snow is blown away from them rather than built up, leaving around the base of every tor a wide scoured-out area. In this wind desert zone the vegetable sheep clump together on an underlay of dead matter, their hairy leaves catching fog droplets. The stunted shrubs are leaf lop-sided, their windblown side unable to grow leaves, and if there is ever a breach in the ramparts and the wind penetrates to the heart, they are doomed.

Insects have stopped bothering to fly, or fly very far. They skip about, short-winged or wingless. Others creep under rocks, hide in bogs, burrow down.

Up here the weather can change in seconds. From out of nowhere great clouds gather, fog thickens, hurricane winds whip, temperatures plummet. It is a place where one can easily lose one's bearings.

*

In the 1940s an attempt was made to harness the slopes into a major ski resort. In a postwar project of great fervour, vision and voluntary labour, three lodges were built near the summit, including Big Hut with bunks for seventy. For some years it was used by plucky parties of downhillers and langlaufers, but by 1954 the heyday was over, the wind had won, and the huts fell into disuse and disrepair. One disappeared. And apart from the odd scientist gauging water on tussock or catching daylight moths, for the next fourteen years this great heap of schist was pretty much left to its windy self.

Until my father came along and made it his ruling passion. For what seemed like every weekend he left home and disappeared up the Rock and Pillar. He sometimes took my tweenage brother, and occasionally some other unsuspecting soul, but mostly he was on his own.

Up and down he went. Up the fenceline to the massive tors, down the slippery snow tussock. Up to the vistas at the summit plateau, down to the paddocks in the valley below; up to the alpine tarns, down to the peaty river; up to the gale, down to the stiff breeze. Lugging his pack. Once he watched as it rolled a thousand metres back down.

He'd arrive back Sunday evenings, late, cold, stiff—and nearly always with horrible tales of weather, accidents, ill-equippedness. Our low-level worry became inflamed when he was overdue, but otherwise we didn't take too much notice. He'd muck-spread about the bags of collected specimens for sorting; the airing cupboard filled up with mosses and liverworts; things were pinned, mounted, boxed, shelved. He'd lose himself peering down a microscope, drawing, identifying by mandible or capsule, fathoming what were often freaks of nature.

*

Come Saturday he sets off again, fossicking about, scrambling across to a different ridge, glissading down a slope, getting caught in fog. He commandeers Big Hut, once he finds it. The chimneys are broken, one corner has slumped, some asbestos sheeting is disintegrating and the ingenious complicated plumbing system has died. But he does a few quick repairs, lugs in some diesel he finds outside, drip-feeds it through the ceiling and gets the old stove going. He shovels out the snowmen that have drifted inside and sets up the ping-pong tables. He sticks his name on all the top lockers, throws some lumpy mattresses over the odd wooden chair-frames, cranks up the gramophone and puts on Dinah Shore: 'Skylark'.

When he loses a crucial bit of his burner and has to make a fire, he burns the wooden scraps of old ski tow and other stuff lying about that doesn't look important. He forgets essentials—matches, food, pieces of equipment. He notices the skies closing in but ignores it just a bit too long. He takes long shortcuts. He loses stuff: the Pentax, the Nikon, his brother in the fog one night. He can't resist wandering off at dark to see what emerges, what nocturnal creatures survive the relentless tugging and tearing of the mountain winds. Numerous cockroaches, large slugs and the handsome mountain rock wētā are out grazing on the lichen fields.

He's beguiled by bog life: the flower-adorned clumps of *Donatia novae-zelandiae*, larvae in their lumpy bejewelled cases, mayfly nymphs. And great expanses of fructifying mosses: *Bryum, Dicranaloma, Lycopodium*.

He swoops around with a net. He sets stations of pitfall traps —Gregg's coffee jars filled with diluted formalin with a dash of detergent, buried up to the brim and protected against rain and snow and direct sunshine by pieces of schist, wedged firmly in the form of a gable. He catches a spectacular bright green wingless stonefly: *Stenoperla prasine*. He finds some tiny short-winged and wingless insects, and discovers two new species of caddisfly which someone names after him—something or other *childi*. Pairs of pipits and dotterels doggedly try to decoy him away, doing that broken-wing thing. Skylarks hover in the foehn winds, inexhaustibly trilling.

He keeps diaries, journals, notes, records; he draws his own maps, makes up toponyms. He sketches out the bogs and flushes, the humps and hollows, and adds in the plants and insects. He paints the landscape in watercolours, all brown and beige. The wind eludes capture. But the journals are full of it: 'Suddenly much darker—dense cumulus cloud blotting out the sun and wind blowing in violent gusts—abandoned investigations' or 'impossible to breathe

in strong wind—very disconcerting.' 'Wind blowing at violent persistent fury—
crawled to hut.' 'Blowing a gale at the top and bitterly cold. No sign of life—not
a lark or an insect dares to emerge in this.'

*

I am off. I will search for *Periwinkla childi* larvae in the waterfall halfway down
Snake Gully. I will fossick about in the tarns and turn over rocks looking for the
slightly curved horn-shaped cases.

I will trample over the *Celmisia* and breathe in the scented leaves. I will
hunt out the carnivorous sundew patch, and the bright red orange drupes of
Coprosma pumila. I will look for the *Dracophyllum* with its leafless windward
side and the small blue and white grass lilies. I will sit on a dense sward of
snowbank plants, listen out for larks, chew on bog pine. I will marvel at the
robust *Umbilicaria* lichen attached to the schist by strong cords.

I will stop on the wide slump of earth interrupting Deep Gully and forcing
the stream to go underground, and watch the awkward craneflies blunder about
in a jungle of vegetation with their long legs trailing. I will poke under rocks for
mountain wētā, frozen solid but still alive.

I will find the small pond below Stonehenge with its fringing of cushion
plants, and look for the intricately intertwined Gordian worms and caddis
larvae. I will seep into bog, be flushed by wind.

I am ready to be delighted by the sight of a fruitfly on a snow patch.

And maybe something will rouse my memory of the one time we did all go,
but truly, sadly, oddly, I have scant recollection of it. We must have all traipsed
up, looking for a good spot—our father collected into a heavy-duty plastic bag
inside a labelled box. But where did we agree, 'This will do'?

I only remember the mad confused gusts of wind. And the ash on our
clothes, in our hair.

FIONA CLARK

Off by Heart

*For though reading seems so simple—a mere matter of knowing the alphabet—
it is indeed so difficult that it is doubtful whether anybody knows anything about
it.* —VIRGINIA WOOLF, from 'How should one read a book?'

Every year around April, members of the American National Association for
Poetry Therapy gather together to discuss poems and how to heal people.
In 2018 they met at a conference centre outside Minneapolis, Minnesota.
According to the association's homepage, even in ancient Egypt people
consumed poetry for their good health: '[W]ords were written on papyrus and
then dissolved into a solution so that the words could be physically ingested
by the patient and take effect as quickly as possible.' The premise here is that
reading, writing and eating poetry are good for you. The conference is attended
by therapists, doctors, nurses and librarians.

Meanwhile in London, Alain de Botton's School of Life offers bibliotherapy:
you go in with a problem and come out with a book. Or more likely, a list of
books that will serve as a prescription for your life. You fold up the bit of paper
with the list on it and put it in your jacket pocket. You whistle all the way down
the street, kicking the leaves off the footpath into the gutter. You go home
and put the bit of paper on your bedside table, or on the floor next to a pile of
half-clean clothes and mugs and unread things. When next you feel bereft or
morally uptight you scramble around for the bit of paper, go to a bookshop
or turn on your Kindle and buy the recommended texts, desperately applying
the words like an ointment to your spiritual and psychological wounds. The
School of Life's prescriptions are made by qualified people who, freed from their
careers in narratology or library collection development, can finally make sense
of where text meets life.

They ask a series of questions: What is challenging you? What is causing you
existential pain? Why is your mind preoccupied by thoughts about a speech
your wife gave at a wedding seven years ago? Perhaps you can reveal that you

have no sympathy for the erotic in contemporary life: dick pics just don't do it for you. You can't get aroused. They might respond kindly with a hand on your leg and a simple 'Il n'y a pas de hors-texte.' Maybe you can both share a chuckle about the semantic sexual failures of your text life, or how they've spent seven years studying Derrida just to make a not-very-funny joke that nobody gets. After a period of awkward shared intimacy they prescribe some Tolstoy or some Nicholas Sparks or some Ursula Le Guin—a cocktail of narrative uppers and downers. You catch the eye of someone in the waiting room on your way out— they are hurriedly shifting their jacket to cover their telling copy of Henry James' *The Wings of the Dove*.

What is it about reading and writing that could be therapeutic? James Pennebaker, a researcher and crucial figure in the history of bibliotherapy, determined that narratives helped people make sense of events: narrative coherency grounded his patients because they were able to use stories to plot sense and purpose into what they were experiencing. This is a straightforward proposition: stories define events and tell them in a certain order. On this analysis, reading is a way of deriving comfort by making sense of things. It's also necessary to make a distinction between therapeutic reading and writing and the deliberate nature of the 'self-help' genre: therapeutic texts don't need to be deliberately instructive in nature. Empathy, edification and self-awareness can be the by-products of reading and not the conscious end-goals.

It's true that a story might cause a reader to find empathy with an otherwise inscrutable character. This is the old 'walk a mile in another man's shoes' sentiment we might write about in high school when we are assigned *To Kill a Mockingbird*. Reading about the experiences of others might also alleviate some anxiety about whether it's normal to experience certain emotions, or it might help us to put concrete sense around what we are feeling. Recognising and identifying ourselves in fictional characters is one way to process our internal thoughts. (Reading Paula Boock's *Dare Truth or Promise* in high school, I knew I was reading a love story that I felt curiously invested in, but my deep affinity to the story of two girls in love percolated without much self-awareness, and it would take another seven years for me to fall properly in love with another woman for the first time.)

The pure act of reading—the suspended self-consciousness that happens while you read—erodes the ego and turns off the inner voice. Isn't this the very opposite of what the self-help industry offers? Instead of self-interrogation, reading can propel you far away from yourself. Virginia Woolf, in her essay on how to read a book, insists that a reader must climb right in alongside the writer as they read. In reading, she says, you have to be down in the docks with the criminal as though you, too, are on trial. Only after your reading ends can you come up out of it, look at it anew and become judge and jury.

You stop reading a book and put it down on the counter beside the toaster. You hurry from your house down the hill to catch a bus. You pay the driver. You can't be in a hurry to make sense of it. Just as you are about to push the button for your stop, you remember some string of words and it is only here and now from this safe distance that you're able to proceed with the new business of thinking about what you read, whether you liked it, and what the characters might have to tell you.

When a person sees a therapist for their grief it's not, at first thought, like poetry at all. But the therapist (a reader of sorts) has people coming in and out all day presenting as unique and wordy challenges. Their clients' ailments divide like poetic forms: sonnet is to compulsive disorder as haiku is to anxiety. The therapist waits for the rare case of a Turkish ghazal. As forms are to poems, so human problems take familiar and recognised structures; each person waits to be interrogated, unfolded and spoken back to.

When I saw a therapist for my own grief I had already tried poetry. My fiancé went to live in Sweden. After a year of long-distance hurt she rang to say she was moving to Italy to be a clerk in a library. We broke up. I drove in a daze the eight hours north to my parents' house. In my old bedroom I found two abandoned banana boxes full of poetry books. I'd bought them in my years at university and as a single, serious poetry reader. I put the boxes in the boot of the white Toyota we'd imported together from Japan and I drove them all the way to Wellington. Driving around the edge of Lake Taupo I heard the books sliding back and forth on the corners, as though just warming up. At home they tumbled from the box, lining up on the shelf. When she and I first met I had stopped reading poetry. Just as suddenly, when our relationship of eight years ended, I started again.

Every night I read from a collection as if I'd emerged, starving, from the woods. On point, I read Carol Ann Duffy's collection *Rapture*, where in 'Forest' you'll find the line:

I followed you in,
Under the sighing, restless trees and my whole life vanished.

I read all the books from school: Eavan Boland, Fleur Adcock, Andrew Motion. I read the poems from the books I started buying in my twenties when I found my own taste: Jackie Kay, Kenneth Koch, Anne Carson, Sharon Olds—collections I picked up when I spent all my weekends scouring second-hand bookshops:

When you and I were first in love we drove
to the border of Connacht
and entered a wood there.

The devoured books built up in piles beside my bed. When I found a poet I'd forgotten I loved, I'd go to the central library and take out more of their books. I started extravagantly and erratically buying paper books again. I was reading them on buses, in the town square on my lunch break, or aloud to myself when I was at home alone in my new flat.

But the familiar haunts of words could not staunch the tears, and after six months of poetry I got out of bed and went to see a therapist. Just a therapist. There was no poetry in her office. She had one distractingly large book on the shelf about losing your family pet. The rest of the books were studious texts. We covered off various therapeutic activities and ideas that came with irresistible names: Karpman's Drama Triangle, Recognition Hunger, The Stroke Economy. Instead of going home and working on practical exercises to help teach my brain the new and healthy habits of a mended heart, I'd go home and research the names of psychological games my therapist had me unpack: Schlemiel, Uproar, Let's You and Him Fight, Wooden Leg. All were tiny poems to me: eclectic words perfectly placed to surmise an entire emotional world.

Eric Berne, the psychoanalyst who fathered the therapeutic school of transactional analysis, would become so familiar and fatigued by the names of the psychological games he identified in human behaviour that he abbreviated them: Now Look What You Made Me Do was NLWYMMD. Now I've Got You (You Son of a Bitch) was NIGYYSOB. I started to feel as though I might be able to condense everything I was feeling and not feeling into a small set of letters: IFGABAH (I Feel Gay and Betrayed and Heartbroken) or WHTML (What

Happened to My Life?). While my therapist pressed me to undo the tight and calamitous patterns of thought I had allowed to become habitual, I found solace in these new and beautiful strings of letters.

Poetry therapists are not really interested in finding narrative verisimilitude with a given life. Working in their niche field they wouldn't meet a couple who felt oppressed by the weight of suburban life and tell them to pick up a copy of Richard Yates' *Revolutionary Road*. They wouldn't meet a person who is coming to terms with their identity and recommend they read *Stone Butch Blues* (though reading Leslie Feinberg would never be a *bad* idea). These exercises would be too literal. While it falls under the umbrella of bibliotherapy, poetry therapy is less interested in Pennebaker's narrative sense as a method of philosophical healing, and more interested in the idea that the metaphors, shapes and sounds of poetry help connect people with the emotions they are (or are not) experiencing.

It's this appetite for the *not making senseness* of poetry that needs to be entertained. People get too hung up on the seriousness of poems. Perhaps it's the way they are taught in school: that each poem must be studiously unscrambled like a reverse egg. Roxane Gay says it best when she says she doesn't know anything about writing or reading poetry: 'What I do know is that when I read poetry, good poetry, I forget to breathe and my body is suffused with something unnameable—a combination of awe and astonishment and the purest of pleasures.'

Unlike stories, poems can be memorised and recited back to yourself (or to anyone who feels comfortable around a poem). Some people find poetry uncomfortable. They react to poems the way some guests react to a dog. The poem puts its nose in their crotch and they smile uncomfortably. They might even laugh politely but you can tell that they hate every minute of it. Some people have been bitten or snarled at by poems—as children or in classrooms—and have lived in fear of them ever since. Some people will cross the street to avoid a poem.

But if you like poems they can also provide comfort. Ask a person who knows, such as a person who teaches poetry at a university. One such person I asked said that in times of grief he turns to the poems he knows off by heart: Emily Dickinson's poem 254 ('Hope is a Thing with Feathers'). He returns to the familiar and begins in recitation: Keats, Tennyson, Wordsworth. Poems with pronounced meter. Odes.

A poem can become a prayer. It can provoke a memory of the time it was last read or last spoken aloud. Poetry can fall as empty familiar sounds intoned without any interrogation of their meaning. My mother used to stand in the small kitchen of our house on Benjamin Avenue in Johannesburg memorising poems while she cooked. She'd close the book and recite the lines as she stirred the pot, then open the book again to check herself against the words. Sometimes when I want to truly grasp the meter of a poem I still have to stand up and walk around the room, deliberately taking a new step with each beat. This is how I was taught to understand iambic pentameter.

When you know a poem by heart it's like getting into a well-made bed at the end of the day: you move around and it feels clean, new, familiar. The edges of the words warm in your mouth. One of the most pleasant feelings of all is to stop and read a poem on paper that you have known by heart for years. You see the lines breaking on the page, the geometric spacing of letters. Small words you had remembered wrongly—an extra 'and'. The punctuation makes the poem suddenly heavier, slower, another shape entirely from the poem you once committed to memory. Poems with colons are common offenders:

And if the earthly no longer knows your name,
whisper to the silent earth: I'm flowing.
To the flashing water say: I am.

Knowing this poem by heart, I always recite the last three words as 'say I am' and lose that emphatic pause.

When I read 'Layover' by Robert Hass I think of the friend I know who loves this poem. Without looking at it I recall the image of the man with the monstrous gloves standing on the salted tarmac. Then I read it and although my memory of the poem is very peaceful, I discover every time that it's really about a war. And yet it closes in a moment of pure humanity:

Soft hum of motors stirring though the plane's low, dim fuselage
the stale air breathed and breathing, we have been sharing.

I like reading 'Layover' alone in airports. I once read it in Germany, halfway to Sweden to visit my fiancée in a wild year before she chose another life without me. There is nothing humbler and quieter than to read this poem while you are waiting alone to board a plane. Even if I am reading it quietly to myself I am always forced to end aloud, whispering 'breathed and breathing' and 'sharing' so that my exhalation creates the breath the poem demands of its reader.

*

I'm sitting alone in a pub in Wellington a year after my breakup. A family comes in and sits opposite. The mother has an American lilt and too-big glasses. The father is young and uncomfortable in his body; his jeans in a slouch down to his shoes. Their little girl chooses the game they will play: Connect Four.

'You be the judge, okay?' she says, looking to her mother and then raising a small yellow chip in her hand. The father racks up the pieces and starts the game. The girl, on her knees on a stool, drops her yellow chip down to where she is most confident. The parents sip their pints. The mother sways to the music. The daughter sways alongside her mother. The father drops a quick red chip and connects three.

'You better watch out, missy!' says the mother.

I go to the bathroom. On my way I see the father's face reflected in a mirror. He is concentrating hard on how to let his daughter win the game without making it seem too obvious to her. How Can I Let You Win? HCILYW.

I'm not seeing my therapist any more. On my last day in her office she said some of the words I needed. It was hot that day and we had the fan on. On the street below us a bus vibrated, stationary at the intersection. A man yelled to his friend. The curtain waved and moved the sunlight on the carpet. I felt myself sweating into the armpits of my shirt and I consciously unfolded my arms to say I was *open* and *inviting* before folding them again.

'All that happened,' she said—leaning forward so I could hear her voice over the sound of the fan and the street and the humidity between us—'is that you were in love.' She smiled. I went back to work and these words hummed and hummed inside me all day toward an incantation of understanding and self-forgiveness: the sum total of it all was that I had fallen in love with a person who wasn't right for me, and it had ended.

I don't believe there is anything original about the sentiments of the poems or stories we love the most. They put the words in order for the things we are feeling: our sense of awe at the size and scope of the universe; a scratch of humour; that pulsating dull feeling of aloneness or aliveness. There are good habits of the brain and bad habits. The therapist sits in their office, one breath away from the patient. Everyone is a new and unique poem sitting opposite. She edits and chips away in search of the honed heart. We are searching for the new forms—any words that might bloom in vibrant, unfamiliar ways.

REFERENCES

For though reading seems ... Virginia Woolf, 'How should one read a book?', *The Yale Review* 89, no. 1 (2001), pp. 41–52.

words were written on papyrus ... 'History of NAPT', National Association for Poetry Therapy: https://poetrytherapy.org/index.php/about-napt/history-of-napt/

Alain de Botton's School of Life ... www.theschooloflife.com/london/classroom/bibliotherapy/

James Pennebaker, a researcher ... Janella D. Moy, 'Reading and writing one's way to wellness: The history of bibliotherapy and scriptotherapy' in S.M. Hilger (ed.), *New Directions in Literature and Medicine Studies* (Springer, 2017), pp. 15–30.

Virginia Woolf, in her essay ... Woolf, 'How should one read a book?'

I followed you in ... Carol Ann Duffy, 'Forest', in *Rapture* (London: Picador, 2005), p. 4.

When you and I ... Eavan Boland, 'That the Science of Cartography is Limited', *LA Times*, 19 June 1994: http://articles.latimes.com/1994-06-19/books/bk-5888_1_eavan-boland

Eric Berne ... *Games People Play: The psychology of human relationships* (Penguin Life, 2016).

What I do know is that ... Roxane Gay, 'A place for poetry', in Fred Sasaki and Don Share (eds), *Who Reads Poetry: 50 views from* Poetry *magazine* (Chicago: University of Chicago Press, 2017), pp. 55–56.

And if the earthly ... Rainer Maria Rilke, 'Silent Friend of Many Distances', Poetry Chaikhana Blog: www.poetry-chaikhana.com/blog/2012/04/04/rainer-maria-rilke-silent-friend-of-many-distances-2/

Soft hum of motors ... Robert Hass, 'Layover', in *Sun Under Wood* (New York: Harper Collins, 1996), pp. 25–26.

JOHN ALLISON

The Way It Is

Nothing you do can stop time's unfolding. —WILLIAM STAFFORD

These are winter thoughts, taken with coffee and stillness throughout the chilly morning. Thoughts of friendship and family. Solitude and companionship in myself and in the world. The creek is running audibly by the back of my cottage, now there's been rain. Its chuckling is yet another friendliness. I'm still arriving here. Today it was a new bookcase delivered, my poetry books liberated from cartons stored until now in the cupboard. I keep glancing towards them. I will get up and pick out a volume, turn the pages, hearing voices and passages … The following poem by William Stafford was one I wanted immediately and it's just right:

> *There's a thread you follow. It goes among*
> *things that change. But it doesn't change.*
> *People wonder about what you are pursuing.*
> *You have to explain about the thread.*
> *But it is hard for others to see.*
> *While you hold it you can't get lost.*
> *Tragedies happen; people get hurt*
> *or die; and you suffer and get old.*
> *Nothing you do can stop time's unfolding.*
> *You don't ever let go of the thread.*

I need some poems in the same way I need bread. This is one of them. I read it again, then glance over to the shelves and know I'll be well nourished. During my late wife's illness we created a *to do* list, to prompt us every day to do those things that otherwise get pushed aside, but which are the real things: *drink water/ breathe/ meditate/ read a poem/ sing/ listen to music or to the birds in the treetops/ walk in the forest or the garden/ observe a particular plant/ talk to someone you love …*

It remains an essential list for the health of body and soul. Don't ever let go of the thread—keep noticing these shining beads strung on that thread. This is my rosary. This is my mindfulness practice. I'm finding my way back into these simple acts. Each morning I write, and in the afternoons I walk and work about the place and meet the grandchildren after school. In the evenings, once they've been fed and are in bed, and I've walked back down to my cottage, I become reflective, within the stillness of the valley. The night is silent, but for the after-images of words in time's unfolding …

What is it that continually pulls me away from these places that nourish me, these activities offering solace and acceptance? I know the intrinsic goodness to be found in solitude and silence, yet often visit so briefly, pausing on the threshold … And then I will return to noise—all that noise outside, all the noise inside. Sometimes the outward noise is a choice (talkback radio and music) to drown out the inward noise (the mind's chatter and commentary). This inward noise often is a choice also, to drown out the still small voice that's audible only in silence. Inward noise especially seems to make all else external. Even the Self. For solitude is the sheath of the Self, and silence is the secret (as in 'secreted') substance of the Self …

So what is it? Scar-tissue of loss and abandonment. A hopeless sense of hyper-vigilance, as if that could make any difference. *Tragedies happen; people get hurt or die; and you suffer and get old …*

Memory is my curse and my blessing, imagination likewise. Strangely, both, precisely it seems due to the scarring, culminate in a harvest of joy and gratitude. But only if attention has been paid … It's that old story—the lotus grows out of mud.

So I turn again towards the dark, knowing it as the generative place for insight. A while ago I heard someone who'd researched sleep patterns in pre-industrial societies, talking on a radio programme called *Life Matters*. Reading diaries and journals, he concluded there were two separate periods of sleep each night. Soon after dark, people went to bed and slept for several hours, and were often then wakeful for some time before sleeping again towards the dawn. This wakeful time during the night was used variously—burglars went house-breaking (the word 'burglar' denotes night-time thieves only), lonely men engaged prostitutes, lovers met, poets wrote, those with pastimes passed time, all kinds of people prayed, others reflected upon their lives, while some would dress up and walk abroad, particularly on moonlit nights, greeting one another, engaging in conversation …

As we grow older, it seems as if this pattern of wakefulness might reassert itself. For instance, no longer ruled so strongly by hours of work and timetables and the insistent necessities of life, I wake towards 3am. It is a good time to keep vigil with my beloved dead, also with my conscience. Who else is awake, I wonder? Often I write for a while. I find myself in these reflective reveries.

Nothing you do can stop time's unfolding. But in these periods during the night it is rather time's timeless enfolding, as in the way I'm wrapped up in memories, in the theatre of my Self, watching scenes from my life as though they were of someone else. Again, again. And through it all there is a thread— continuous, coherent. It's always been there, though there were times when it slipped away from my grasp. But mostly now I've got a grip. I realise I long for others to witness this.

These are winter thoughts, accompanying me through my day into the evening and into the night. This afternoon I sat with a friend in a bar, and we talked as we always have talked. Otherwise, not much else happened today— though the bookcase was an event. Do I have to explain about the thread? Is that what I'm writing about? There's a sense of a stillpoint that I've come to, and now I'm talking to myself, telling myself that this is the way it is. After the first reflective thoughts, there's this chatter. For in order to write this, I've come back out into the noise. I talk it through with myself, formulating phrases and sentences, rendering them via the quietly clattering keyboard. I wander back and forth across the threshold of the Self, between reflection and action. In this inbetween place, just here, I'm poised upon a high-wire of thought. And now, for my trapeze act, I swing back out towards the Open …

You don't ever let go of the thread.

REFERENCE
There's a thread you follow … William Stafford, 'The Way It Is', *New and Selected Poems* (Minneapolis: Graywolf Press, 1998).

LOUISE SLOCOMBE

The Thorndon Esplanade

They cannot walk fast enough. Their heads bent, their legs just touching, they stride like one eager person through the town, down the asphalt zigzag where the fennel grows wild and on to the esplanade —KATHERINE MANSFIELD, 'The Wind Blows'

The asphalt zigzag is easy to find. It's just down from the house where Katherine Mansfield was born on Tinakori Road, in the suburb of Thorndon: a short pathway with white wooden railings. There is not much wild fennel these days but there are plenty of other weeds—tradescantia, oxalis, cuckoopint—growing in the shade of some very large pōhutukawa trees. And the wind still blows of course; this is Wellington after all. It is blowing particularly hard today, violent gusts that stop me in my tracks.

But of the esplanade there is no sign. I cannot see the sea, nor can I feel the sea spray, wet and cold inside my mouth, unlike Matilda, Mansfield's adolescent protagonist. Instead, the zigzag path takes me down to Thorndon Quay, a wide nondescript street of furniture stores and offices, quiet on this Saturday afternoon. Instead of looking out over the harbour, I'm looking across the road at a carpark, and beyond that railway sidings, then more carparks and the squat grey cylinder of the Westpac Stadium. Above me is the concrete bulk of the motorway where unseen vehicles rumble overhead.

When I first read 'The Wind Blows' I assumed that Mansfield's esplanade was a fictional creation. The land on the opposite side of Thorndon Quay from where I'm standing, with the carparks and the railway sidings, is reclaimed from the harbour. Before the reclamation, Thorndon Quay used to run along the shoreline (the name gives it away), snaking between the sea and the abrupt hills of Thorndon. There was no space for an esplanade.

But Mansfield's stories, particularly those set in New Zealand, were closely based on her own life. In 'The Wind Blows' the emotionally turbulent Matilda

158

is modelled on Mansfield herself, while the brother who accompanies Matilda to the esplanade is called Bogey, the family nickname of Leslie, Mansfield's only brother. Even the piano teacher, who comforts Matilda a little too solicitously when she bursts into tears during her lesson, is based on a real person. The wind is real of course, and Mansfield's places also had their real-life counterparts. All around Thorndon, interpretive panels mark locations that Mansfield used: the 'little mean dwellings' that feature in 'The Garden Party' (replaced by a cement works that has since been replaced by a vehicle repair workshop); the iron suspension footbridge over a gully mentioned in 'A Birthday' (replaced by the motorway). The Tinakori Road house where Mansfield was born appears in 'The Prelude'. But there are no interpretive panels here on Thorndon Quay and nothing to tell me the esplanade ever existed.

There is photographic evidence, however. In the National Library's digital collection I find a postcard depicting 'Thorndon Esplanade and Baths, Wellington, New Zealand'. Two young women in long dark skirts and white blouses walk down a long straight promenade by the harbour. Behind them is what must be the baths—a large square building with domes at each corner. The women look as if they are holding hands and one of them is holding on to her hat. Their bodies are angled slightly, as if braced against the wind. I find another photograph, dated 1900, where a woman sits stiffly on a wrought iron seat in front of a domed bandstand. A man walks on the opposite side of the promenade, very close to the fence as if he is trying to keep the greatest possible distance from the seated woman, or maybe from the photographer.

I dig some more and find numerous references to the esplanade in digital newspaper archives. I learn that Wellington's harbour reclamations happened bit by bit, the land gradually accreting into the sea. In the early 1880s a small sliver of land was reclaimed alongside Thorndon Quay by the Wellington and Manawatu Railway Company, for the new railway line running to Napier. On the far, seaward side of the railway tracks was a straight strip of land, edged by a sea wall. This became the esplanade, a 'place of public recreation', around the time that Mansfield was born in 1888.

An exposed, dusty track running alongside the railway would not have been much of a place for a seaside promenade. In 1889 a city council deputation approached the country's premier and asked that the esplanade be vested in the council so it could 'plant it with trees and in other ways make it a suitable spot for the recreation of the people'.

But a local resident, George Woodward, was unwilling to wait for the slow wheels of government to turn. He was already working on the wealthier residents of Thorndon, persuading them to pay for twenty wrought-iron seats for the esplanade 'for ladies and invalids'. The seats were to have 'griffins' heads and ornamental tracery work' and each one would bear a plaque recording the name of the seat donor for posterity. Many of the donors were 'identities', people who were considered (or who considered themselves) notable in early Wellington society.

Once the seats had been organised, the 'energetic Mr Woodward', as he was described in the local papers, started raising funds for a band rotunda— another essential requirement for a place of recreation—complete with an 'iron Mosque top' and gothic balustrades. This too would record the names of donors inscribed on 'ornamental brass escutcheons'.

Mr Woodward then turned his attention to vegetation. He started raising money and mustering support for planting trees on the esplanade to mark Arbor Day. He met with scepticism initially—unfamiliar with the US concept of Arbor Day, people thought he was collecting for the Harbour Board and accused fundraisers of poor spelling. But Mr Woodward's efforts paid off and Arbor Day was officially celebrated for the first time in New Zealand with tree-planting on the esplanade. The esplanade may have been one of the first places in Wellington where the now ubiquitous pōhutukawa trees were planted. By now the city council had taken over the esplanade, but Mr Woodward continued to act as the unofficial guardian, writing to the council whenever he felt it wasn't keeping up with maintenance.

Katherine Mansfield would have grown up with the esplanade. It could be seen from the back-bedroom windows of the Tinakori Road house. In 'The Aloe', the esplanade is present at the birth of Kezia, another fictionalised Mansfield: 'The Grandmother shaking her before the window, had seen the sea rise in green mountains and sweep the esplanade.'

Mansfield's real-life grandmother might have wheeled the infant Kathleen (Mansfield's birth name was Kathleen Beauchamp) along its exposed length, perhaps stopping to rest on Mr Woodward's seats. They would have heard the occasional blast from the gun battery on the esplanade, complete with six howitzers and flagpole, fired to salute important ships arriving and leaving, or to mark events of international significance such as the assassination of US President McKinley (when a half-mast Stars and Stripes was flown from the flagpole). As a schoolgirl, Kathleen learnt to swim in the newly opened Thorndon Baths. By the time she was an adolescent, like Matilda in 'The Wind Blows', the esplanade was a highly fashionable place to stroll and cycle. On Sunday afternoons people came from all over the city to listen to brass bands performing in the rotunda. Mr Woodward would have had good reason to be proud.

Every act of creation tells a story, whether an esplanade or a work of literature. The esplanade's story—bare land newly reclaimed from the sea and furnished with the trappings of a nineteenth-century British park—was a small-scale manifestation of the colonial endeavour, creating a Britain of the South Seas in the blank space on the map that was New Zealand. It was also a story about the early settlers' notion of Wellington. When the esplanade was created, there was no shortage of public space, with over a thousand acres of town belt in the hills surrounding the city. But the esplanade was created for genteel promenading, suitable for the inhabitants of the civilised city that Wellington aspired to be. The energetic Mr Woodward, and other creators of the esplanade, were also telling a story about the significance of this far-flung colony to the rest of the English-speaking world. This was a country that played a role in international events, even if that role was mostly limited to firing a gun into the harbour or hoisting a flag. The seats, too, with the plaques celebrating the generosity of socially eminent 'identities', told a story about who was important and deserved to be remembered. Mansfield probably had this sort of thing in mind when she described New Zealand as:

> ... a little land with no history.
> (Making its own history, slowly and clumsily
> Piecing together this and that, finding the pattern, solving the problem,
> Like a child with a box of bricks)

As well as being a slow and clumsy process, making your own history is fraught with problems, not least that it can be undermined by alternative interpretations. A couple of years after the seats were installed, a Major-General

Schaw donated another seat. The major-general wanted to commemorate an act of bravery—that of William John Morris, a ten-year-old boy who drowned trying to save his younger brother who had fallen into the sea from the esplanade. I think of that seat as a silent reproach to the other seats—the heroic sibling who had earned his place in esplanade posterity alongside those self-made identities who had purchased theirs.

Not everyone shared the notion of the esplanade as a place of respectable recreation. Mr Woodward's seats had barely been installed when 'mischievous spirits' had 'commenced disfiguration by carving initials upon them'. Residents wrote letters of outrage to the *Evening Post* about 'yahoos' and 'hoodlums' on the esplanade, and there were complaints about illegal games of two-up, 'pugilistic encounters' and horse, car and bicycle races. The esplanade's location, on the far side of the railway and on the edge of the city, would have made it easier for miscreants to get away with their transgressions.

Promenading was also compromised by the new city's lack of infrastructure. Early Wellington was notorious for poor sanitation (Katherine Mansfield's sister Gwendoline died from cholera in 1891 at the age of eleven weeks), and residents frequently complained about bad smells on the esplanade and about sewage finding its way into Thorndon Baths. A 1907 visitor from Christchurch wrote to the *Evening Post* about dead dogs and 'also a pig or two' lying on the beach near the esplanade.

But the main impediment to creating an esplanade in the image of a genteel resort on the south coast of England was that Wellington is *not* like the south coast of England—or anywhere in England for that matter. The early settlers had already made this mistake—sailing into the harbour, clutching their plans for a city set out on an orderly grid surrounded by gently rolling hills planted with wheatfields, to be met with the cruel reality of rugged hills and steep-sided valleys, extreme winds, earthquakes and flood-prone rivers. The esplanade (perhaps itself a hankering after that lost city of gracious boulevards) was in a particularly exposed location, and would frequently have been blasted by the weather that Mansfield described in 'The Wind Blows'. Fashionable ladies would have had to contend with the wind thrashing their skirts around their ankles, their best Sunday hats careening over the harbour. Band concerts were often cancelled due to the weather and the wind stunted even the hardiest plants—in

'The Wind Blows', Mansfield wrote: 'all the poor little pahutukawas [sic] on the esplanade are bent to the ground'. There must have been days when the esplanade was deserted, apart from the odd adolescent letting off steam after a close encounter with a piano teacher.

Mansfield's esplanade is not Mr Woodward's esplanade. While she may not have been among the miscreants who irked the more genteel promenaders, she was a rebellious spirit, pushing against the constraints of Wellington society. In 'The Wind Blows' Matilda has been unsettled all day by the wind, which has stirred up strong emotions and sexual desires. She is alone in her room feeling edgy and afraid when her brother appears and suggests they go down to the esplanade. Once they are there, the wind becomes a source of exhilaration and the esplanade becomes a place offering possibility and escape. They watch a steamer leaving the harbour, and then time seems to flip. Bogey and Matilda are on the steamer leaving Wellington, and remembering 'the esplanade where we walked that windy day'. It is unclear whether Matilda is imagining her future or whether the siblings on the esplanade have been revealed as a memory. Either way, at the end of the story, time has dissolved, the ship has gone and only the wind remains. The esplanade is a transitional place where future freedom can be imagined or experienced, and the present can become the past, like a long hall of mirrors sliding in and out of different points in time.

'The Wind Blows' was inspired by conversations between Mansfield and her brother. In 1915 Leslie had enlisted in the British Army and often stayed with Mansfield at her London home while training nearby. That October, shortly after 'The Wind Blows' was first published, Leslie was killed in France. Mansfield was devastated. She decided to write about New Zealand as a memorial for Leslie: 'I feel I have a duty to perform to the lovely time when we were both alive. I want to write about it and he wanted me to. We talked it over in my little top room in London.' She set out to recreate the New Zealand places she had experienced with Leslie: '… in my thoughts I range with him over all the remembered places. I am never far away from them. I long to renew them in writing.'

Like the Wellington colonists, Mansfield was making her own history by recreating her past, full of people and places she knew. But her narrative, focused on family life and relationships, on domestic interiors, on fleeting impressions of light and the weather, was very different from the colonial narrative.

The esplanade would have been fixed in Mansfield's memory during the height of its popularity. Shortly after she left Wellington in 1908 it entered a long decline. In 1910 further land reclamations were carried out to expand the railway. The waters of the Thorndon Baths were muddied by silt from the reclamation works and new railway lines cut across part of the esplanade. The increased numbers of trains would have created more smoke and noise. By the time that Mansfield was writing 'The Wind Blows' on the other side of the world, bands no longer played in the rotunda, Mr Woodward was dead and the planting was no longer being maintained. In 1917 the council declared it could not justify 'spending a penny' on maintaining the esplanade due to uncertainty about future expansion of the railways. It had become 'an uncared-for, desolate patch' where children no longer played. Avoided by respectable society, it was frequented by lovers lingering after dark on Mr Woodward's seats.

By 1918 its fate was sealed. There were to be further land reclamations on the seaward side and the story had changed. Nothing must 'stand in the way of national and district advancement,' said the mayor, and the esplanade had to be sacrificed.

The short life of the esplanade runs oddly parallel with the short life of Katherine Mansfield. Created the year that she was born, its decline mirrored the decline of Mansfield's health. She experienced her first symptoms of tuberculosis a few years after leaving New Zealand and died at the beginning of 1923—the year that work began on the reclamation that subsumed the esplanade.

Standing at the bottom of that asphalt zigzag in the wind, I can't let go of the idea that there must be something here still, some physical sign, or even just a fleeting sense of what the esplanade might have been like. I can't retrace its course, forever buried under out-of-bounds railway land, but I can try to get as close to it as I can. I set off up Thorndon Quay, peering into the gaps between the furniture shops, the wind harrying me from behind.

When you make your own history, you choose what to include and what to leave out. It's not just the esplanade that is missing here. Mansfield's 'little land with no history' did of course have a history, a history that was known, treasured and recorded. Right here on Thorndon Quay was a sandy beach called Te Oneihaukawakawa. At the other end of Thorndon Quay was Pipitea Pā. A stream called Whakahikuwai ran through the gully behind the house where Mansfield was born, and entered the harbour just about here. A little further on another stream called Tiakiwai ran past two kāinga up on the cliffs and then down into the sea. There is no sign now of either stream, not even a damp patch on the footpath.

Wellington's original shoreline was a source of food, a place to land canoes, and held cultural and spiritual significance for the people who lived around the harbour over hundreds of years, most recently Te Āti Awa and their allies who were here when Europeans arrived. Their shoreline was obliterated by the esplanade and successive harbour reclamations, and their cultivations and pā were taken and built over by European colonists. By the time the esplanade was created, most of those Māori who hadn't succumbed to European-introduced diseases had left the area.

I turn off Thorndon Quay and into the vast brick railway station, completed in 1937 on reclaimed land. You can no longer take a passenger train from here to Napier and the scale of the station is out of all proportion to the few suburban lines it now serves. At the end of the platforms, ramps lead up to the Westpac Stadium concourse. I battle my way across its white concrete expanse, leaning into the wind, and look down on the railway lines. This is the closest I can come to the physical space occupied by the esplanade. The long straight concourse is rather esplanade-like—you can at least see the wind-chopped sea from up here. The stadium was built in the late 1990s, on land no longer needed for the railway. Oversized and minimally roofed, it offers little protection from the elements. Crowd numbers have been declining recently as the stadium struggles to compete with live sport on TVs in comfortable living rooms and bars, and it is frequently compared unfavourably with the new roofed-in stadium in Dunedin. The esplanade was a blip in the short history of Wellington, and the things that succeeded it have themselves been supplanted.

From the stadium I go down to Aotea Quay, a bleak busy road that runs alongside the port. Cruise ships dock here, and the *Emerald of the Sea*, its flags stretched taut by the wind, is preparing to set sail. I scan the rows of identical balconies, looking for an excited Matilda and Bogey dreaming of the past and of the future, but there are only a few middle-aged couples here and there braving the weather for a last look at Wellington.

I cross the bridge over the railway and return to my starting point on Thorndon Quay. Tired from the wind, and depressed by my surroundings, I feel annoyed with myself. What did I expect to find? And why does it matter that an esplanade existed here once and has now disappeared without trace?

The short life and obliteration of the esplanade is unsurprising given the dizzying pace of change over the relatively short period of time since Europeans arrived here. This is the colonial endeavour: a succession of building and demolishing, rebuilding and demolishing, exploiting resources and abandoning them. When I was looking for some sign of the esplanade I was looking for some material evidence that told a story, something that connected this place to the past and could connect me, the lone walker in the wind, to this place. It is stories, after all—personal memories, shared histories—that connect us to place. But in this succession of demolition and rebuilding, the layers of stories have no opportunity to accumulate. When things change so quickly, how do you choose what to remember and what to forget?

In the absence of anything else, it's easy to fall back on glib hashtags, or to let others—usually the corporate marketeers these days—tell our stories about the places where we live.

The esplanade has an enduring presence at least in 'The Wind Blows', even though it only appears as a bit-player at the end, woven into Mansfield's fabric of recreated memories of Wellington people and places. She once wrote: 'We only live by somehow absorbing the past—changing it—I mean really examining it & by dividing what is important from what is not … & transforming it so that it becomes part of the life of the spirit and we are *free of it*.'

In 'The Wind Blows' the esplanade lives on, just as Leslie Heron Beauchamp lives on as Bogey, but 'transformed' by Mansfield into its essence—or at least its essence for her, as a wind-blasted transitional space where you might feel free. In the end, it is this kind of story that tells us about where we are—one that seeks to understand and even to transform, but not simply to impose.

Before it handed back the esplanade to the harbour board, the council frugally relocated Mr Woodward's seats to parks around Wellington, including the Botanic Gardens. Unable to relinquish my search for material evidence, I scour the Gardens one hot sunny day, the postcard image downloaded on my phone, looking for the distinctive griffins' head ironwork. There is no sign of them, and I become increasingly dispirited and overheated. This is, of course, another futile expedition. It is highly unlikely the seats would have survived the extremes of the esplanade and then lived on for another ninety years. I imagine them rusting out their days behind a council potting shed, their corroded intricacies a danger to tiny fingers.

But then, on my way out past the soundshell lawn, I find two of them side by side. I sit down and run my fingers over the fierce little griffin heads with their pointy ears and gaping jaws. There is no sign of the plaques with the names of the 'identities'. Then I find another seat. This one has pride of place in the white gazebo by the main path and it still has its plaque—not of the name of a puffed-up colonial identity, but the memorial plaque for William John Morris, the boy who was drowned trying to save his brother in the harbour waters near the esplanade.

REFERENCES

A place of public recreation … The Thorndon Esplanade Act, 1891(3).

Plant it with trees … 'Deputation to the premier', *Evening Post*, 16 March 1889.

For ladies and invalids … *Evening Post*, 18 June 1889.

Griffins' heads and ornamental tracery work … *Evening Post*, 8 August 1889.

Iron Mosque top … *Evening Post*, 22 October 1889.

Ornamental brass escutcheons… ibid.

a little land with no history … Katherine Mansfield, 'To Stanislaw Wyspianski', in Gerri Kimber & Claire Davison (eds), *The Collected Poems of Katherine Mansfield* (Dunedin: Otago University Press, 2016), pp. 103–04.

I feel I have a duty … Katherine Mansfield in Margaret Scott (ed.), *The Katherine Mansfield Notebooks* vol. 2 (Wellington: Daphne Brasell Associates, 1997), p. 16.

… *in my thoughts I range* … ibid., p. 32.

Spending a penny … 'The esplanade at Thorndon: Policy for the future', *Evening Post*, 16 February 1917.

Stand in the way … 'Big schemes', *Evening Post*, 11 October 1918.

We only live … Katherine Mansfield to John Middleton Murry, 30 October 1920, in Vincent O'Sullivan and Margaret Scott (eds), *The Collected Letters of Katherine Mansfield* vol. 4 (Oxford: Oxford University Press, 1996), p. 90.

P.J. STANLEY

Anatomy of Belief

The story I'm about to tell is normally played out in reverse. Parents, concerned for their son or daughter who has suddenly become different and has cut off contact, desperately try to rescue them. There's always anguish, there's always a change in personality, there's always blame and loss. These things are ascribed to involvement with a cult, brainwashing, and subjugation to some sort of charismatic leader. My story is something I'll be coming to terms with forever, sifting through the anatomy of belief, looking for the key to understanding a drive that seems more powerful than the parental love that is supposed to last a lifetime.

My dad cut all contact with me a month after my son was born. He's never met his grandson. His only grandchild. He has no intention of ever speaking with me again. If I try to call him, he ignores me. My dad is seventy-six years old and I'm his only child. He's a smart guy, has a PhD in physics from Stanford. We'd always been close, had a good, open relationship. But now, he won't even have a conversation about why he's cut me off. I don't know if I'll ever properly understand. This is the cost of religion, of beliefs that transcend family.

It happened on a Monday. My son was three weeks old exactly. That morning he was downstairs with his dad. I was sitting in bed with the dappled sunlight playing across the geometric bedspread; there was a curious contentment in having time alone. I slipped into the new normal, the new routine, reaching to the bedside table for the breast pump. There was a tiny human who needed me and his needs came first. Always. The ritual was automatic. Attach, switch, increase pressure, pump. Close eyes. Breathe. In. Out. In. Out. Relax.

The email from my dad sat at the top of the inbox on my phone. I felt a lift to see his name. I opened it smiling, the metronome of the pump continuing in the background. It was strangely formal in the salutation: 'Dear daughter,' it said. I hadn't heard from him in a couple of weeks but that wasn't unusual—he was often travelling. I wondered where he was. Working? Attending a course in some exotic location?

I could hear my husband talking to my son, playing with him. Milk gushed into the bottle as I thought of them both. I was still recovering, developing as a new mother. I was just beginning to cope, to adjust, to settle into a life where everything looks different. Slowly I was coming to terms with the new identity I had to assign myself. My old identity was subsumed by the perfect tiny human we had created.

I read the email, breasts attached to the pump, naked in bed, and my world dropped away. Snippets reverberated around my head as my phone fell to the bed and tears dripped onto the mechanically grinding pump. 'No further contact' … 'until the situation changes' … 'wish you all the best'. In a curious mixture of a greeting card gone wrong and a breakup letter my father had broken up with me, and in doing so he broke me.

How could he do this to me? What has happened? The thoughts tumbled over themselves. *Was it me? Was it because of Mum? Did they tell him to? Why now? Why?* Tears arrived along with the thoughts that will never leave me. *What did I do wrong?* The questions seemed to grow, to bounce inside me. The email gave no reasons.

My husband heard me crying and hurried in, carrying our son in his arms. 'What's wrong?' he asked frantically. Later he will say he wondered if it was postpartum depression setting in. Or news of a death. It might as well have been. Shaking, shell-shocked and heartbroken, I gestured towards the phone on my lap. All the while the pump continued in the background, expressing, draining, filling the bottle, drop by drop.

The reality of it thumped away in my head with the same remorseless rhythm. *He loves his religion more. He'll never talk to you again. You're not that important. He loves his religion more. He'll never talk to you again. You're not that important.* It became a mantra, all I could think about.

The news travelled around the rest of the family quickly, and rallying cries were issued:

'Oh the stupid bastard.'

'I could kill him.'

'How could he?'

'It's not really him, he's brainwashed.'

'If he does that you've lost him already.'

'You've done nothing wrong.'

'We will always love you.'

'That stupid religion really is a cult.'

'You don't want him if he's like that.'

'He loves you really, underneath it all.'

'It's not your fault.'

All true. All supportive. All symptomatic of the type of love that I have lost from him. But none of it helped. I couldn't find the words but the thoughts were fully formed. I had been betrayed by one of the two people in the world who are supposed to love me unconditionally. The foundations everything was built on were shaken. The city of my life had developed, grown, far outstripping the original city walls, but it all stemmed from the love of the two people who created me and held me first.

My son blinks at me. Too young to smile yet. He is totally dependent.

Will I ever email my son to tell him he is out of my life? The thought is ridiculous. Farcical. Ludicrous. Words are insufficient to describe the insanity of the thought. I was still laying the first stones in our son's foundations, loving him unconditionally, being everything for this beautiful and dependent tiny human that I have helped to create. I was busy building his fortress while my own was ransacked from the inside, destroyed by the gatekeeper. I was destroyed.

Anger. How could he do this by email? The coward. It's one thing to be manipulated by belief but another to lack the convictions of your beliefs. I'll call him, I thought. Then he will have to consciously ignore me. Why should I make it easy?

My husband held me helplessly as the tears fell and the thoughts ran through my head. The bedspread had reversible zigzags I never noticed before. I felt the anger resonating from the tension in the arms around me. My husband could not protect me from this.

'Do you want to talk?' he asked.

'I don't know,' I mumbled.

'Why? That's the thing I don't understand. Why would he do this?'

'There's a policy, a rule. They must have told him to do it.'

'So, what, he'd jump in the lake if they told him to?' His anger bubbled over.

'Disconnect. That's what they call it. They have a whole teaching, policy and writings on how to deal with such situations. If people are antagonistic towards them or question the truth then they disconnect.'

He looked at me incredulously. How could I explain it to him? It made it sound as though I was defending it. I hate it.

They supervise the process, read the letters and coach the respondents so that they cannot be talked around by emotion. My email, that formal email starting with 'Dear daughter', had been written and supervised. It was from them, not just from him. Even this was controlled. Was this the last contact I would ever have with him?

My father died that day. He's alive though. He eats, sleeps and breathes. He cut himself from the photograph of my life and now there's a hole that can't be filled. Perhaps given time the edges will blur and the background will fade into the gaping space. But the negative has been damaged and my vision of the world irrevocably altered.

I should have seen it coming. Hindsight, irritatingly smug with its clarity. What were the warning signs I missed? The thoughts thumped endlessly, in bitter juxtaposition with the innocence of my newborn son. Your dad loves his religion more. He'll never talk to you again. You're not that important. He loves his religion more. Then the refrain of the lost: 'If I'd known then what I know now …'

It's funny how memories are mental snapshots. What is it that sears one ordinary moment into the retained consciousness and deletes the surrounding ones? For so many years I'd thrust the memories away, deeper, hiding them. I dusted them off, an archaeologist looking for ancient faultlines to make sense of the changing sands beneath me.

*

At first glance, getting involved with a cult is anathema to the Kiwi archetype. We're chilled out, laid back, we've got a 'sweet as' mindset that never gets too involved in anything emotive or fringe. Religion, yep, that's all good, save it for Sundays though, mate. We don't have that problem of weird religions and people being separated from their families. We're a land of middle-of-the-roaders; cults are for other countries, excitable Americans. Well, apart from those Gloriavale weirdos we laugh at on the telly, but they're not really a cult, just hard-core Christians. They're on the West Coast, too; much easier to make jokes about because they live over there. Good fodder for Jonno and Ben on a Saturday night.

I don't think I've ever had a conversation with a Kiwi friend about religion. But if you scratch the surface there's a lot of variety out there. There are more than a few cults, too, and not just the ones that make the news. We talk a lot these days about racial identity, about how colour and culture define who we are. The polyglot country we're evolving into accepts those different identities as part of a patchwork forming one continuous entity, like the Canterbury Plains seen from above. Beliefs are more amorphous, harder to detect; there are often few external markers and their effect is not easily seen at first glance.

I grew up in New Zealand, went to a conservative private school in Christchurch and attended chapel once a week in school time. Granddad had a farm. We can trace our ancestors back to those lauded 'First Four Ships' and there are streets and markers around Canterbury that carry my forebears' names. In those respects, our family is as Kiwi as can be. Sunday family roasts, pav at Christmas, gumboots and jandals and good yarns. We're the archetype. But we Kiwis are not all mildly lackadaisical Anglo-Christians.

Scientology. Yes, that one. Tom Cruise jumping on couches, Xenu the master lord (the only place I've heard that is on the internet) and myriad other oddball rumours and appearances. I grew up travelling to the headquarters of this so-called 'religion' every year. That's the thing about religion—some people find it, or are found; others are just born into a reality that assumes a state of normalcy. My parents met through Scientology. I was brought up as a Scientologist. Until I was in my early twenties I considered it something I believed in. I suppose you could call me an accidental Scientologist. Now lapsed. Very lapsed.

The trouble with being inside something is that your view becomes warped, refracted by the influence of people close to you.

What is a cult? What is it about the word that is so emotive? At what point does a differing belief outside the mainstream qualify as a cult? There are academic studies and the internet abounds with opinion pieces, but none capture the emotional trauma of the reality of something ephemeral that entraps the people you love.

Trauma is the clearest marker of when something is destructive as opposed to just a little weird. They'll cut you off from your family and friends; the belief, the organisation *always* trumps every other relationship. And to achieve that end there are rewards and consequences—rewards if you stay close and report others, and consequences if you step out of line. The threat of disconnection from the people you love is a powerful one, and this cruel policy is enforced by the Church of Scientology. If someone disagrees with the church then they are 'suppressive' and you must 'disconnect' from them. If you don't, you are expelled.

Shades of Orwell's *1984*.

I'm a heretic, apparently.

In New Zealand most of our religious sects have a Christian base. There's a fascination with them and they make good media fodder. Gloriavale, the Exclusive Brethren, the rather catchy God Squad, Jehovah's Witnesses, Destiny Church, Mormons. There's a sense that although they may be extreme in some of their beliefs they are basically okay, not dangerous. Who hasn't heard of Dove Love? They're weird, sure, but in New Zealand we don't really go in for that cult stuff they have overseas, right?

It's interesting, delving into the Kiwi psyche just a little bit. DIY is in the archetype, right up there with 'she'll be right' and number eight wire. There's something in our make-up, in that outdated and increasingly inaccurate umbrella definition of 'real Kiwi' that's a by-product of living far from civilisation and needing to be innovative as settlers. We're beginning to acknowledge that there's a strong indigenous influence on that archetype, that Māori values and beliefs are instilled in the psyche too. The idea of a religion or belief system that offers practical solutions can be seductive to that psyche. A cults offers something new, something that will bring great change. That's the draw.

Growing up, I never thought there was anything too odd about my parents being Scientologists. But then again, I didn't think about it much. It was something we did when we went overseas, something I could ignore when we came home. Holidays were twice a year to Florida, to Scientology headquarters.

Florida—pretty lucky, right? High school made me more aware. Conservative Christchurch. Private school, chapel once a week and twice a term on Sundays. How did I fit into this? Was I now an accidental Christian? Those were hard questions to contemplate as a thirteen-year-old trying to find her place in the world.

My parents split when I was eight. Dad had always been travelling and in hindsight, the writing had been on the wall for ages. The great thing was that they were Scientologists, which meant they were able to stay friends and everything was easy. That was how it seemed when I was eight, and for a long while afterwards.

When I was sixteen I left school and went to America on holiday. I signed up, joined the Church of Scientology. I was convinced I was doing something with purpose, something meaningful. The contract I signed was for a billion years. I lasted two. Let's look at that again, though. I was sixteen years old. I moved to America on my own, and signed a *billion*-year contract. I look back now in utter disbelief.

I lived in a two-bedroom flat within a Scientology compound with eleven other people. My bed was in the dining room. There were three in the tiny lounge and four in each of the two bedrooms. We shared one bathroom. We worked six and a half days a week from eight in the morning until ten at night. Saturday mornings we got off to do laundry.

I got in a bit of trouble early on. I came home to New Zealand to sort out my affairs and kissed a boy I knew. Yes, just a kiss. I was sixteen and a half. When I got back I had to confess. I was told I was depraved and degraded, and busted down to kitchen duty. Ironically, that worked out well for me. I managed to learn how to cook and walked away with a skill that was useful in the real world.

The full story is a little more complex but I was controlled more and more, prevented from contacting my family, paid only $40 a week and had my passport taken away. Looking back, I'm amazed I got out.

*

Six months before I got married my dad called me to tell me he was disconnecting from my mother. He would never talk to her again. Through my tears I asked him why. Though divorced for twenty years they had stayed friends. They used to call each other and talk about all sorts of things, not just me. Dad lived overseas and when he came to visit me he stayed with us—with my mum and stepdad. It was weird, but for me, good.

After we talked he agreed he would talk to my mum for the day of the wedding. That was all.

My big day. Dad walking me down the aisle with my stepfather, an arm each. My dress was perfect—a plunging heart-shaped neckline and delicate straps made out of the finest French lace. The wind blew my veil out behind me and pressed the dress to my body. We married outside, under snow-capped mountains with a lake in the distance. Our wedding was perfect. And yet as I walked down the aisle towards Mum with the two men I call Dad, both of whom I love dearly, I knew this was the last time I would have my parents together.

I asked him the question the next day. Would he ever disconnect from me? I made him promise he wouldn't. He hesitated but he did it, he promised. Later he said he did it because he didn't want to upset me. He waited through my whole pregnancy because he didn't want to upset me and put me in any medical danger. He saved it up until a month after I gave birth.

*

Freedom of speech means that we can't legislate against harmful cults and beliefs—nor would I advocate any such restriction. That would be hypocritical. We're an island sitting proudly in our corner of the South Pacific. That lends itself to a lot of isolationism. Keep your weird religions overseas. If you're going to bring them here at least have the grace not to talk about them. Especially if you're trying to persuade me to go along. No way, mate. Clear off.

I'm a parent now with no particular belief. Not in formal religion. If pressed I would speak to a belief in some greater force, something beyond us that I don't feel the need to define any further. I believe in family. I believe in love. I believe in being open-minded.

I will never force my son to believe, or disbelieve, in anything. I won't try to restrict him. I will raise him to question intelligently, to look at things before him and measure them against a yardstick of fairness. Does the belief system seek to separate him from his family? Does it squash all questioning? Is it litigious? If the answer to those questions is yes then I hope he will have the sense to walk away.

*

It's worst at night time. I lie in bed sometimes, unable to sleep, and think of all the questions I want to ask my dad. I'd just like him to explain why his religion is so important to him, why the man in the picture, holding me as a newborn with his lips tenderly pressed to my forehead, no longer wants to talk to me.

I don't think I'll ever get over it. Being a parent has made it worse. I couldn't imagine ever leaving my son. The thought thumps away at my head: 'He doesn't love you enough.' And so my heart cracks again, silently. So many things make a sound when they break, but the most precious thing of all fractures silently, holding the pain inside. I have been abandoned by my father, one of the two people who were supposed to offer unconditional love forever. In some ways it's worse than a death. What will I say to my son when he is old enough to ask about his grandfather?

About the Editor

Emma Neale has published six novels and five poetry collections, and edited several anthologies. She is a former Robert Burns fellow (2012) and has received numerous awards and grants for her writing including the Janet Frame/NZSA Memorial Prize for Literature (2008) and the University of Otago/Sir James Wallace Pah Residency (2014). She was the Philip and Diane Beatson/NZSA Writing Fellow in 2015. Emma received the 2011 Kathleen Grattan Award for her poetry collection *The Truth Garden*, and was a finalist for the Acorn Foundation Fiction Prize at the Ockham New Zealand Book Awards 2017 for her novel *Billy Bird*, which was also longlisted in the International Dublin Literary Awards 2018. She holds a PhD in New Zealand Literature from University College London (UK).

Since 2018 Emma has been the editor of *Landfall* journal. *To the Occupant*, her latest collection of poems, was published earlier this year.

Contributor Biographies

John Allison is a poet and prose writer whose fifth collection of poetry, *A Place to Return To*, was published by Cold Hub Press in mid-2019. During the 1990s he had poems, short stories and essays published in numerous literary journals here and overseas. 'The Way It Is' comes from an essay sequence titled *Cancer Chronicles and other Familiar Life Stories*. After fifteen years in Melbourne John returned to live near Christchurch in 2016.

Jane Blaikie is a Wellington writer and editor. Her collection of poems, *Tongue Burglar*, was published by Steele Roberts in 2018.

Tobias Buck studied art history and creative writing under Gregory O'Brien at Victoria University of Wellington before completing a postgraduate degree in the US and a master's at the University of Edinburgh. He has worked in digital media and publishing in London and Auckland, and at independent bookshops in London, Rio and Melbourne. Alongside owner Tilly Lloyd, Tobias project-managed the recent redesign of Unity Books Wellington. In 2014 he won the BNZ Katherine Mansfield Prize for his story 'Islands in the Stream'.

Madeleine Child lives in Dunedin. She has a couple of sons and a dog and makes things. For the past few years she has been trying her hand at writing, and is surprised to find it not so very different from working with clay. Her work has appeared in *Landfall*, *Bonsai* and *Bath Flash Fiction*.

Fiona Clark currently lives and works in Wellington. She completed her MA in English literature at Victoria University of Wellington in 2009, and an LLB in 2019. She has previously lived in Johannesburg, London, Edinburgh and Kyoto.

Sam Keenan lives in Wellington. Her work has appeared in *Cordite*, *Landfall* and the *Poetry New Zealand Yearbook*. She was runner-up in the 2017 *Sunday Star Times* Short Story Competition.

Cait Kneller writes and sells books in Auckland. Her work has never appeared in print before, and may never again …

Jessica Maclean is a seedling of Ngāti Kahu, Ngāti Hine, Clan MacGill-Eain and Clan Ó Eaghra. Borne along by various winds and tides, she came to rest in Ōtautahi, where she has remained since.

Becky Manawatu is of Pākehā and Māori (Ngāi Tahu) descent. She was born in Nelson in 1982. Her first novel, *Auē*, was published by Mākaro Press this year. She is a reporter for *The News*, Westport. Her short story

'Abalone' was long-listed for the 2018 Commonwealth Short Story Prize. She has work published by The Spinoff and the online literary magazine Headland. Becky gained a diploma in writing for creative industries from the Nelson Marlborough Institute of New Zealand.

Alice Miller's collection of poems, *Nowhere Nearer*, was published by Auckland University Press and Liverpool University Press (2018). She lives in Berlin.

Mikaela Nyman is a New Zealand writer born on the Åland Islands in Finland. Her work has been published in *Sport, Turbine, SWAMP, JAAM, Sweet Mammalian* and *Minarets*. Her first poetry collection (in Swedish) was published in Finland in April. She is completing a PhD at the International Institute of Modern Letters at Victoria University of Wellington and writing a novel concerned with women's voices in Vanuatu. Her latest work involves a series of collaborative poems with Ni-Vanuatu writers.

Jocelyn Prasad has lived in Australia for eleven years but still calls New Zealand home. 'Uncut Cloth' started off as an essay about sarees but ended up as a story about her mother and growing up in Mount Roskill. She is trying to write a novel about an Indian woman who travels to Fiji, her parents' homeland, in the early twentieth century as an indentured labourer. 'Uncut Cloth' was first published in *North & South* and has also appeared in *Meanjin*.

Derek Schulz is a poet, essayist and writer of fictions. He was the recipient of the 2018 Caselberg International Poetry Prize.

Tracey Slaughter won the 2015 *Landfall* Essay Prize with 'Ashdown Place'. She is the author of the highly acclaimed collection of short fiction *deleted scenes for lovers* (VUP, 2016), and a poetry volume *conventional weapons* (VUP, 2019). Her poetry and short stories have received numerous awards, including the international Bridport Prize 2014. She teaches at the University of Waikato where she edits the literary journal *Mayhem*. This essay was written for the 2018 symposium 'Writing Matters'.

Louise Slocombe writes about places and journeys, both real and imagined. She moved to Wellington from the UK twelve years ago and has been exploring it ever since. Louise has an MA in creative writing from Nottingham Trent University and her work has been published in New Zealand and overseas.

P.J. Stanley is a short story and non-fiction writer who has been published in *North & South* and online in Headland, The Spinoff and Newsroom. She was educated at the University of Canterbury and taught secondary school for ten years. In 2019 she completed a master's in creative writing from the University of Edinburgh, and is currently working on a novel set among the wild landscapes that underpin the Kiwi psyche.

Tim Upperton's second poetry collection, *The Night We Ate the Baby*, was an Ockham New Zealand Book Awards finalist in 2016. He won the Caselberg International Poetry Competition in 2012 and again in 2013. His poems have been published widely in New Zealand and overseas, and are anthologised in *The Best of Best New Zealand Poems* (2011), *Villanelles* (2012), *Essential New Zealand Poems* (2014), *Obsession: Sestinas in the twenty-first century* (2014), and *Bonsai: Best small stories from Aotearoa New Zealand* (2018). An extract from this essay appeared on NZ Poetry Shelf, edited by Paula Green, in February 2019.

Kirsteen Ure grew up in Port Moresby and has also lived in Auckland, London and Hong Kong. She is a graduate of the University of Auckland's Creative Writing Master's programme. In 2018 her work was awarded Headland literary journal's Frontier Prize and was long-listed for the Takahē Monica Taylor Poetry Prize.

Susan Wardell is from Dunedin, where she lectures in social anthropology at the University of Otago, while raising two small humans and a few potted plants. Along with an academic book, articles and blogs, she has published poetry in *Landfall*, *takahē*, *Not Very Quiet* and *Plumwood Mountain*. She won first place in the 2019 international 'Micro Madness' competition, and also the 2019 Maxim Institute essay competition.

Bryan Walpert is the author of three poetry collections, most recently *Native Bird* (Mākaro Press); a short story collection, *Ephraim's Eyes*; and the scholarly books *Poetry and Mindfulness: Interruption to a journey* and *Resistance to Science in Contemporary American Poetry*. His essays have also appeared in Australia and the US. He is a professor of creative writing at Massey University, Auckland.

Justine Whitfield is originally from Porirua City and now lives in Nelson. Her writing has appeared on The Pantograph Punch, kiss me hardy, Headland and in the Nelson Arts Festival. 'The Klimt Bubbles' was first published by kiss me hardy in November 2018.